BRUNEI

for my always-supportive parents, David and Louise

BRUNEI
The Modern Southeast-Asian Islamic Sultanate

by

David Leake, Jr.

McFarland & Company, Inc., Publishers
Jefferson, North Carolina, and London

The assistance of Prof. Alan Howard of the University of Hawaii at Manoa in creating the maps in this volume is gratefully acknowledged.

British Library Cataloguing-in-Publication data available

Library of Congress Cataloguing-in-Publication Data

Leake, David, 1950–
 Brunei : the modern Southeast-Asian Islamic sultanate.

 Bibliography: p. 161.
 Includes index.
 1. Brunei. I. Title.
DS650.3.L43   1989   959.55   89-42730

ISBN 0-89950-434-5 (lib. bdg. : 50# alk. paper) ∞

Printed in the United States of America

McFarland & Company, Inc., Publishers
 Box 611, Jefferson, North Carolina 28640

Contents

v

Introduction

The government bureaucracy of the tiny oil-rich sultanate of Brunei is huge, employing close to one-seventh of the population. It is structured along thoroughly British lines but tends to operate in ways distinctly Bruneian. I was never more aware of this fact than during my last 24 hours in Brunei, when the government effected a radical transformation of my life although I had only fleeting contact with a single bureaucrat, the airport immigration official who checked my passport as I left the sultanate for good. I found it amusing that my first intimation of my impending expulsion came from one of the drivers of the company I worked for, who heard about it from an Immigration Department clerk he met in a coffee shop.

I arrived in Brunei, on the northwest coast of Borneo Island, in March 1981 with my Malaysian (now ex-) wife to work as one of two sub-editors on the weekly *Borneo Bulletin*, the sultanate's only newspaper, which is published in English with a small Malay language section. Due to the lack of qualified local residents, the paper's publisher, Brunei Press Limited, must import most of its small editorial staff. Most other companies in Brunei requiring specialized personnel — notably Brunei Shell Petroleum and its many contractors — must likewise recruit overseas. As a result, there is a large stratified expatriate community, with the upper administrative level dominated by *orang puteh* (literally "white men" in Malay) whose presence has stimulated the opening of small supermarkets and various shops catering to their tastes. Most of these enterprises are run by commercially oriented Chinese immigrants, who maintain an uneasy symbiotic relationship with the numerically and politically superior Brunei Malays.

To understand modern Brunei requires an appreciation of its ethnic realities. It has been ruled by Brunei Malays for just about all of its known history, yet the local economy is now Chinese-dominated. The government naturally slants its policies to benefit its Brunei Malay power base; most of the Chinese have found it impossible to gain citizenship in their adopted land and are therefore stateless. The promotion of Islam, the national religion, is also used to strengthen traditional Brunei Malay culture and maintain ethnic unity. There are various other indigenous groups, both Islamic and non–Islamic, but they play minor roles due to their small numbers and positions on the economic and political periphery. More important are the *orang puteh*, most of whom find Brunei to be a tropical paradise.

Although the name Borneo tends to evoke images of wild men in an untamed jungle, this part of the world's third largest island is well developed, with paved roads, clean piped water, electricity, and all the other amenities taken for granted in modern industrialized nations. Expatriate residents can pursue their favorite sports, ranging from golf and snorkeling to cricket and tippling, year-round. Oil industry wages and benefits are substantial, while the cost of living is generally much lower than back home; most *orang puteh* households can readily afford the less than $250 per month salary of a full-time *amah* (female servant).

Brunei is ruled by a Brunei Malay sultan who holds autocratic powers, but his use of them must be described as benign. The security forces maintain a lower profile than in some of Southeast Asia's ostensible democracies. Nearly all *orang puteh* make it through their stays in the sultanate without any hassles with officialdom, largely because they live within the cocoon of Brunei Shell Petroleum Company, a virtual state-within-a-state which has long dominated the oil industry. Despite the insularity, there are occasional incidents of *orang puteh* offending the powers that be, knowingly or unknowingly, and being punished. I heard one story of how an oil worker aggressively overtook a car which happened to be driven by a district officer (administrative head of one of Brunei's four districts), who was so angered he arranged to have the offender expelled.

But the *orang puteh* are generally welcomed, if for no other reason than that the all-important oil industry could barely function without them (a situation which has naturally been fostered by the imported administrators themselves). In many Third World nations, Westerners are viewed with an ambivalent mixture of admiration for the social and material progress of their home countries and distaste for their real or imagined assumption of superiority. In Brunei, however, the positive feelings tend to outweigh the negative. An important historical factor is that the British helped to preserve the sultanate without quite colonizing it, and established a bureaucracy that is now a downward conduit for a substantial portion of the nation's oil wealth. Part of this wealth has financed the overseas higher educations of thousands of Bruneians, who usually have positive experiences during their stays in Britain, Australia, the United States and other Western nations. Additionally, the gulf between the living standards of most *orang puteh* and Bruneians is not so great as to engender widespread intense envy.

On the other hand, within some sectors of the populace resentment is openly expressed about the privileged position of the foreigners and the way Western culture threatens to overwhelm the traditional Brunei Malay one. One reaction has been a growth in demands for the Islamization of all aspects of life, but these have been only partially satisfied since many influential Muslims oppose them. It has also been enshrined as government policy that citizens (Brunei Malays foremost) will gradually take over the top administrative and technical positions now held by foreigners and resident Chinese. Those with the right connections may rise faster than their skills warrant, but generally it is a gradual, pragmatic process requiring workers to have proper training and sufficient experience before they are promoted.

It will be many years before Brunei Malays are really dominant in their own oil industry and in other fields requiring specialized skills. Such is the situation at the *Borneo Bulletin*, where the editorial staff remains predominantly Western. I first arrived in the region through stints as a U.S. Peace Corps volunteer in the two states of East Malaysia which, along with Brunei, were once collectively known as British Borneo (Malaysia's 11 core states constitute the Malay Peninsula across the South China Sea). I occasionally submitted captioned photos and short feature stories to the *Bulletin* about interesting people and practices I came across, which led to my job on the paper. The editor was a gruff New Zealander who was fairly adept at taking stories just as far as the government would tolerate.

My arrival in Brunei coincided with increasing attention from the foreign media due to the approach of "full" independence from Britain, on January 1, 1984, after nearly a century as a protectorate. The British press, which is often highly irreverent towards its own royalty, showed particular interest in Sultan Sir Hassanal Bolkiah's status as supreme ruler and world's richest man (as he may rightly be dubbed if his control of Brunei's purse strings is taken to mean he can treat the national wealth as his own). The point was sometimes made that something must have gone wrong if all those years of British tutelage had failed to bring about a parliamentary democracy with budget-making out of the hands of royalty.

The Information Department was obviously ill-prepared to deal with the flock of foreign print and video journalists who suddenly began nosing around. There were virtually no briefing materials to hand out, and the available statistics were generally outdated, which only increased the flow of distorted impressions and shallow analyses often produced by journalists who catch their stories on the run. I thought I might be able to capitalize on the growing interest in Brunei by writing a few articles from the vantage point of a resident able to speak to the Brunei Malays in their own language (thanks to my Peace Corps experience), and presumably with a more realistic grasp of the situation than transient journalists could gain.

My first submission of this sort was my last. A relevant bit of background information is that I had devoted much of my spare time to photographing Brunei, not only for the fun of it but also in hopes of supplementing my income. It seemed to be a saleable topic: I met a well-known American freelance photographer who was drawn to Brunei by the advent of its independence, and there were probably others I did not run across. A photo stock agency in New York City expressed interest in seeing my photos, so I culled the best from among 1,200 or so color transparencies and put them in a pair of cardboard packets. In one of the packets I also enclosed an article providing an overview of Brunei as it approached full independence, since this stock agency also peddles photojournalistic pieces.

Before mailing the packets, it occurred to me they might be suspicious-looking enough to warrant postal inspection. I had heard incoming mail was routinely opened but I made the apparently unwarranted assumption that outgoing mail was less likely to be inspected. The Brunei government never stated why I was being expelled, but I later learned that such matters come under a national security committee, which took exception to something I had written for overseas publication. I suspect it was the article sent with the photographs (which did reach their destination), even though it was never published, since its slant on how the sultanate's oil wealth is apportioned was unflattering. I should have mailed it separately in a less conspicuous envelope.

One mid-morning late in November 1983, about two months after mailing the offensive packet, I left my desk to check on how one of my page layouts was being handled in the production room. There I met one of the drivers, who mentioned that an Immigration Department clerk had told him in a coffee shop that there was some "problem" with my passport. He did not say what the problem was though he certainly knew it was insoluble — in fact, I would not be surprised if most of the coffee clientele in the quiet little town of Kuala Belait knew a *Borneo Bulletin* staffer was being expelled before I did. An hour or two later the Brunei Press general manager called me into his office after getting the official message over the phone from the head of the local immigration office: my passport was to be turned in to be stamped with the words *Di-arahkan keluar* ("Ordered to leave"), and I had to be on a plane out of Brunei the next day. But I did not have to endure a berating, or even a didactic lecture, from a representative of the sultan.

In Singapore, I collected my final paycheck and air tickets home from the Straits Times publishing organization, then the majority shareholder in Brunei Press (members of the Brunei royal family are now the principal owners). My unspecified, presumably subversive activities made me a liability, a threat to the substantial flow of profits for the Straits Times from Brunei (since the *Borneo Bulletin* is the only print advertising venue there, and a major one as well in East Malaysia). The Straits Times tried to cast me out of the region altogether by maintaining I had to accept air tickets straight back to the United States, but I managed to get a set via Kota Kinabalu, the capital of the East Malaysian state of Sabah, where my wife was from. There, I landed another editorial job on a daily newspaper, and was able to keep in touch with events in nearby Brunei.

This book is intended to provide an overview of the sultanate, past and present. It was not written in a way meant to exact revenge for my expulsion. That was something I was readily able to put behind me, since I accepted I would have to live in Brunei according to its rules and knew the risks associated with breaking them.

The first half of the book covers Brunei's long and interesting history, which can be traced back more than a millennium. The landmark switch to an Islamic sultanate came close to five centuries ago, after which a Brunei empire was forged, sprawling over most of Borneo and neighboring islands. Then, as today, the primary residential community was built on stilts over the Brunei River. However, internal dissension and encroaching Europeans led to a steady decline, which would probably have resulted in the sultanate's obliteration but for the British taking it under wing in 1888. About 40 years later it was shown that, remarkably, the shrinkage of the sultanate still left it sitting atop some of the region's richest petroleum deposits.

The second half of the book examines modern Brunei, which is in an expansionist phase by virtue of one of the world's highest per capita national incomes. The present sultan is the twenty-ninth in a royal line that some scholars believe goes back more years than any other in the world. His government, dominated by his own relatives, uses petroleum revenues to finance such a high standard of living for residents (largely as a way of heading off discontent) that the sultanate has been called "the Shellfare state." The oil wealth is also being invested in business ventures all over the globe, by royal family members using their personal fortunes and on behalf of all citizens by the Brunei Investment Agency. On the surface, Brunei appears to live up to its official title of the Abode of Peace, yet there are unresolved tensions related to race, religion, and the autocratic system of government, and there is also the riddle of how to diversify the economy away from total dependence on a dwindling resource. How these problems are dealt with will determine whether the new Brunei commercial-financial empire will continue to rise or go into decline.

I

The Water City,
Heart of Empires

Visitors to Brunei are invariably fascinated by Kampong Ayer (meaning "water village" in Malay), a sprawling community of nearly 30,000 people who live in houses built on stilts over the Brunei River, just next to the rapidly growing and traffic-clogged capital, Bandar Seri Begawan.

The water villagers, who are mostly Brunei Malays, get around via zippy outboard-powered boats or plank walkways. Bread-winners typically hold office jobs and drive to work in air-conditioned cars they park overnight on the river bank; in the evening, they are likely to join their families watching video cassettes if the scheduled color television shows don't suit their taste.

There are "kampong ayers" in many parts of coastal Borneo, but Brunei's is unique not only for its large size and modernity, but also for its long history as Brunei's former capital and one of Southeast Asia's most important ports. Indeed, both the water community and the empire of which it was the heart were long known as either "Brunei" or "Borneo" — variations of a word apparently derived from the Malay word *berani*, meaning brave. In this historical account of Brunei, Kampong Ayer's forerunner will be referred to as the Water City to better reflect its size and importance.

Ancient Empires

Chinese and Arabian texts over 1,000 years old have been found describing a kingdom — centered at a water community — that may well have been Brunei's precursor. There is, for example, a work called *'Ajaib al-Hind (Wonders of the Indies)* written by an Arab sea captain around 950 A.D. He describes a place called Sribuza, which Robert Nicholl, an expert on Brunei history, thinks may have been located on Brunei Bay and ruled

1

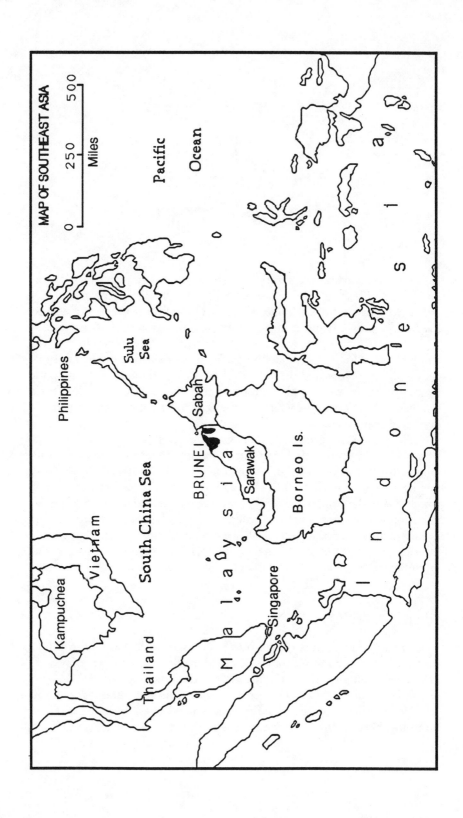

by members of the Royal Family of Funan (in the area of present-day Kampuchea) who were driven from the mainland by the Khmers during the seventh century (the Funanese were seafarers, like the Bruneis).

On the basis of reports from other seamen, the Arab wrote of Sribuza:

> There is no bay larger in the whole island. The tide is felt every 12 hours. Crocodiles are found there, but those which are in the part which adjoins the houses do not harm, having been bewitched, as we have said, whilst those parts situated away from the buildings are unapproachable, by reason of these creatures.
>
> Some houses are built on land, but the greater part float on the water, sustained by pieces of wood tied together to form rafts, which last forever. They do this from fear of fire, for their houses, being built of wood, are much subject to conflagration, and fire once having taken hold, burns furiously. Placed on the water, the houses are better protected: if fire breaks out at one point, each householder can cut his moorings and make off going away to settle somewhere else far from the blaze. If he is unhappy with some particular place, he can move to a different quarter of the town.
>
> These houses in the bay are arranged in such a manner as to form streets. The water between the houses flows abundantly. It is fresh water, which comes from the uplands to enter the estuary, and flows into the sea in the same manner as the Tigris.

There is strong evidence that Arabian, Indian and Chinese traders had already been coming to Borneo for centuries to carry away its exotic jungle treasures — camphor, rhinoceros horn, edible birds' nests and much more. That there was an ancient "trading kingdom" at Brunei is indicated not only by such writings as the Arabian one quoted above, but more concretely by archaeological excavations. For example, the radiocarbon dating method suggests that Chinese ceramic trade wares and coins found at Terusan Kupang, about three miles upriver from Bandar Seri Begawan, date from as early as A.D. 750. There are also indications of iron smelting. It appears this site was abandoned around the end of the thirteenth century, after which the focus of trade shifted to Kota Batu, about seven miles downriver.

In China, many texts survive that pertain to trading activities in ancient times, and some of them undoubtedly describe the main trading centers along Borneo's coast. The problem is identifying which Chinese names stand for which locations, and this has generated much disagreement among scholars. Some, for example, believe that Vijayapura, which existed some 1,400 years ago, was the same as the Sribuza described above and was located on Borneo's northwest coast, possibly at present-day Brunei. But others consider the west coast more likely. Vijayapura was noted by the Chinese to have been highly developed socio-economically, although it did not trade directly with China at that time.

Map of Southeast Asia, showing location of Brunei.

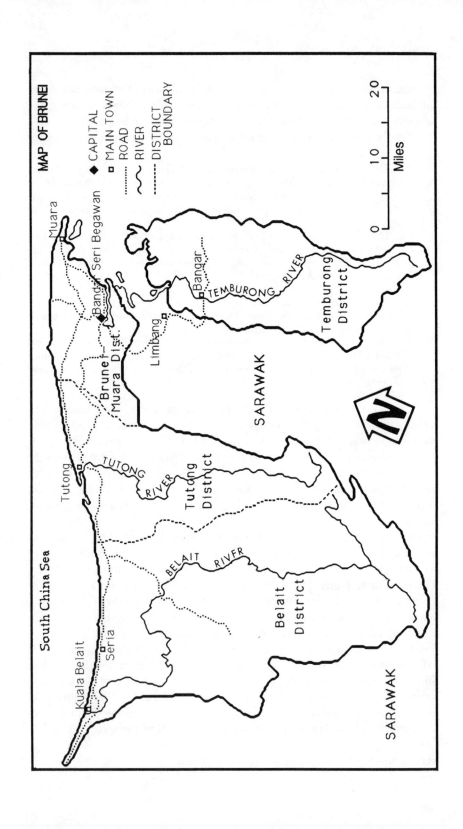

Another possible Brunei forerunner is Po-ni, a Chinese name not so far in sound from "Brunei" since the character "po" was also used to represent the first syllable of "Buddha." This place was mentioned by the Chinese as early as the ninth century. Many scholars feel confident in equating Po-ni with a water community on Brunei Bay, based on the location, climate, produce and customs of the Po-ni described by the Chinese. However, these same descriptions could arguably apply to other parts of Borneo, although Brunei remains the leading contender.

In Robert Nicholl's estimation, there were three empires which the Bruneis were able to forge because they were very close-knit and were also able seamen whose war fleets could ward off enemies and intimidate vassal states, and whose far-ranging trading ships brought in riches.

The first empire would have included northwest Borneo up through the Sulu Archipelago (the southernmost islands of the Philippines), and its most important produce would have been camphor, the crystallized sap of the *kapur* tree. Northern Borneo has long had the reputation of producing the world's finest camphor, which was once worth more than its weight in gold due to Chinese and Indian belief in its curative properties. It appears that down through the ages lower-grade camphor was generally sent to India, while the best quality went to China, where it fetched fabulous prices (the Chinese term for it translates as "dragon's brain").

The Sumatran empire of Srivijaya apparently conquered that early Brunei's dominions in the early ninth century, for it was then that Srivijaya was said to have taken control of the camphor trade of "Tawaran" (presently Tuaran in Sabah). There followed about 150 years during which Brunei's trade with China was, remarkably, totally cut off due to Sumatran control. However, Srivijaya lost its hold over northwest Borneo in the late tenth century due to warfare with the Javanese which forced it to pull its warships back from the South China Sea. This allowed the Bruneis to resume trade with China and set about building their second empire, which the Chinese knew as Po-ni.

Nicholl estimates that this, one of Southeast Asia's biggest empires, held sway from about 1000 to 1350 and included present-day Sabah, Sarawak, and the Philippines. The king of Po-ni sent tribute missions to China in 977 and 1082, but after that there was a gap of about 200 years, perhaps due to Po-ni's own might (it has been suggested that it successfully resisted conquest by the Mongol empire-builder, Kublai Khan, who succeeded in pillaging Java in 1293).

While Brunei seems to have been known as Po-ni to the Chinese, the Arabs apparently called it Muja. Al-Idrisi's *Book of Delights*, written in 1154, describes Muja as producing the world's best camphor, and also as

Brunei today.

engaging in piracy. The pirates were known for their bravery and were led by a "pangan" (Brunei *pengiran* — member of the royal family) wearing a gold collar. The men under him were dark-skinned with matted hair, apparently sea nomads who were subservient to the Bruneis in return for protection.

Chinese accounts told of a great water city, but it appears to have been at the mouth of a river — probably the Lawas — on the other, eastern side of Brunei Bay from present-day Kampong Ayer. The reason for supposing this is that the Chinese said there was a large range of mountains behind it, and tall mountains do indeed spring up in the Lawas interior.

Life in Po-ni

An account of Po-ni was written around 1225 by Chau Ju-Kua, controller of customs at the port of Ch'uan-chou in Fukien Province. Based on the reports of others, he described it as the most important port in the "Eastern Ocean" (the Moluccas, Sulu, north Borneo and south to Java) and as having the region's most highly developed government, which strictly controlled trade over a large area. Significantly, he said it was the main source of the very best camphor.

As for life in Po-ni there were some interesting tidbits:

> The king's residence is covered with *pei-to* leaves; the dwellings of the people with grass.
> They use the floss of the *ki-pei* plant to make cloth. They draw the sap from the heart of the *wei-pa*, the *kiamong*, and coconut trees to make wine.
> When the children of rich families married, the presents began with wine, then betelnuts, then a finger ring, and after this a gift of cotton cloth or a sum of gold or silver, to complete the marriage rite.

Po-ni's military might was represented by more than 100 warships. The ruler was said to be borne about in a litter, accompanied by more than 500 men with those following carrying delicacies on gold platters. Gold items were said to be abundant, and there was even "melted gold colored silk" (*kain songket*, the cloth patterned with gold or silver threads which is still standard ceremonial wear in Brunei as well as Malaysia).

But Brunei's glory was to fade rapidly, for sometime in the 1300s it lost its possessions to the Java-based Majapahit Empire, which rose after Kublai Khan's expedition and maintained good relations with China. A Javanese document called the *Negara-Kertagama* and dated 1365 listed one of Majapahit's tributary states as "Buruneng," which almost certainly referred to Brunei. And four years later this shrunken state suffered the indignity of being sacked by former subjects, the Suluks of the southern Philippines (who were later to be subjected by a revived Brunei but then regain their independence again). It took a Majapahit rescue fleet to drive out the Suluks, who were said to take with them two giant pearls from a Po-ni temple (the presence of these pearls, and the popularity of the "flaming pearl" motif on tombstones in ensuing centuries, leads Nicholl to suggest that the Po-ni of that period was Taoist).

The subsequent decline of Majapahit set the stage for Brunei to again take full control of its own affairs and turn to empire-building. An important turning point may have come just after the founding of the Ming Dynasty by Hung Wu. According to the official history of the Dynasty, in 1370 he sent envoys to Java who then stopped at Po-ni, asking the king to send tribute to their emperor as Majapahit had itself become a tributary of China. The Po-ni king pleaded temporary poverty due to the recent Suluk attack, but he did finally agree to send the requested tribute.

The benefits of good ties with China for Po-ni were probably that it escaped the control of declining Majapahit earlier than it would have otherwise, and also gained lucrative trading links with which to rebuild its wealth and, consequently, its military might. The king of Po-ni again sent tribute in 1405, and three years later visited China himself with a 150-strong entourage that inclined his wife, children and younger brothers and sisters. His aim was apparently to secure Po-ni's full independence from Majapahit, and it appears this was gained even though he died in China itself about one month after his arrival.

This was the period of the Yung Lo emperor, who ruled from 1403 to 1425. The Po-ni ruler, called Maharaja Karna, was received with great honor at the imperial capital of Nanking, about 120 miles from present-day Shanghai. On his death following an illness, the emperor ordered a special royal tomb and associated temple to be built 15 miles southwest of Nanking. As well, an impressive series of stone statues, one-third larger than life, were erected in pairs along either side of an avenue leading to the hill in which the tomb was set. These statues, which had fallen down and been overgrown, were rediscovered and set upright by researchers from the Nanking Museum in 1958. They consist of two horses, two grooms, two rams, two lions and two generals, plus a tortoise with an inscribed tablet on its back. The magnificence of Maharaja Karna's tomb indicates how highly the Chinese regarded Po-ni.

According to the Ming history, the emperor decreed that Maharaja Karna be succeeded by his son Sura Wangsa, who although still just a boy apparently attained his father's wish for Po-ni's independence. Sura Wangsa told the emperor that tribute had hitherto been paid to Majapahit, and asked that this be diverted to China instead. This request was granted, and the emperor also declared that Po-ni should have a state mountain — a distinction shared only with Japan, Malacca and Cochin. So the Po-ni visitors returned home with an inscribed stone to be set up on what would be known as the Mountain of Lasting Tranquility Preserving the State (presumably in the Lawas interior, if the Po-ni capital was indeed on the Lawas River). Although that stone tablet has never been found, Po-ni came to be known to the Chinese as the Country of Lasting Tranquility, which was translated in Arabic as Darussalam (Abode of Peace) — and this name remains as part of Brunei's official title.

The severing of the Majapahit connection greatly reduced the influence in northwest Borneo of Indian civilization (which contributed Hinduism as Majapahit's way of life). This influence had been felt for hundreds of years — as indicated by archaeological finds of Indian artifacts at Santubong and Limbang in present-day Sarawak — and indeed many of Brunei's titles, ceremonies and customs have a distinct Indian element. As well, ancient tombstones can still be seen in Brunei bearing Sanskrit inscriptions.

The Coming of Islam

But the predominant influence for at least the past 500 years has been Islam which, as the Majapahit Empire fell, was rapidly gaining followers in coastal areas throughout Southeast Asia due mainly to the proselytizing of Muslim traders from the Middle East and even China. Muslims came to power in Java, Sumatra, the Malay Peninsula, and Sulu, and before long Islamic sultanates dotted the coast of Borneo.

According to the royal genealogy in the annals known as the *Selasilah* (Book of Descent) — said to have been commissioned by the fourteenth Brunei sultan, Muhyiddin — the pagan ruler Awang Alak Betatar converted to Islam and became Brunei's first sultan. He is said to have married into the royal family of Johor (at the southern tip of the Malay Peninsula) and to have gone there for his installation as sultan, after which he took the name Muhammad. His gifts from the Sultan of Johor included a large portion of northwest Borneo (the five "states" of Sambas, Kelaka, Sarawak, Samarahan and Sadong) and the *Gunta Alamat*, consisting of musical instruments which could be played only for royalty.

Just when this took place, however, remains very much a subject of debate among scholars, who have come up with dates more than 200 years apart due to different interpretations of the scanty surviving written and oral records (the scribes of ancient Brunei wrote on thin tree bark which was unable to survive the centuries). In 1515, for example, the Portuguese in Malacca noted that Brunei traders said their ruler had only recently converted to Islam. Other documents, however, indicate that when the survivors of Magellan's world-girdling fleet limped into Brunei Bay in 1521, either the fifth or the sixth Muslim sultan was on the throne. On the basis of this and other evidence, it has been suggested the first Muslim sultan was installed even before 1300. But it has also been pointed out that Chinese accounts of Maharaja Karna's visit in 1408 make no mention that he was Muslim, which would have been expected to be of great interest to them. Neither was his tomb built in line with Islamic custom. Yet Stamford Raffles in his *History of Java* records that Brunei's "Rajah Chermin" (the third sultan) had visited the Rajah of Majapahit and tried to convert him to Islam, which must have come no later than the early 1400s.

One fascinating suggestion that could explain these contradictions is that the decline of pagan Lawas-based Po-ni while under Majapahit allowed the rise of a rival Islamic state on the other side of Brunei Bay, up the Brunei River, which eventually supplanted Po-ni altogether. One supporting bit of evidence comes from Pigafetta, the Italian chronicler of Magellan's fleet. He wrote that on Brunei Bay there was "another city inhabited by pagans, which is larger than that of the Muslims, and built like the latter on salt water. On that account the two peoples have daily contacts together in the same harbor. The pagan king is as powerful as the Muslim king, but not so haughty, and could be converted easily to the Christian faith." None of Magellan's men, however, actually visited that other water city.

Whatever year may mark the beginning of the Islamic sultanate, it is generally agreed that the first sultan was Muhammad. This is the name given by both the *Selasilah* and the various versions of the ancient epic poem called the *Sha'er Awang Semaun*, which describes the origins and development of Brunei and was orally handed down over the centuries.

The Egg-Borne God

The poem begins by telling how a huge egg descended from Kayangan (heaven) and landed in the upper Limbang River (a part of Brunei until the end of the last century). After a long time, the egg divided into four parts and a young man emerged—Sultan Ahmad Dewa Emas Kayangan, who was to father the originators of the royal line which rules Brunei to this day.

American anthropologist D.E. Brown, an authority on Brunei's history and socio-political development, speculates that the huge egg was the same as the *Hiranyagarbha* (Golden Egg) of Hindu mythology, in line with the strong influence Indian civilization once exerted throughout Southeast Asia. Sultan Ahmad Dewa Emas Kayangan would then be equivalent to Indra, the Hindu king of gods; "Dewa Emas Kayangan" means the "Golden God from Heaven" and Indra is identified with gold (and red). The significance of this connection is seen in long-standing beliefs among the people of Borneo that Brunei's sultans had magical powers, for example the ability to bestow fertility. Brown notes that the Bruneis may have seen their ruler as a "conduit for a life-giving force" and adds, "To this very day Bruneis regard their sultans as possessors of magical power."

The "Golden God" from the egg married a Murut woman in the upper Limbang area, but he departed when she was three months pregnant, leaving behind a ring and a note of explanation. He had many adventures and married a total of 14 women (seven and its multiples hold magical connotations for many Borneans) in the region of Brunei Bay—leaving each one with a ring and a note when she was three months pregnant.

Each of the 14 bore a son. The eldest began searching for his father but stumbled on the second-born, identified by the note and ring. Eventually all 14 brothers and their father were reunited. After a period in Kayangan, the brothers returned to Earth and began to build a kingdom, choosing Awang Alak Betatar from among themselves as their leader because of his superior qualities. The brothers and their followers introduced many of Brunei's customs and established their capital-on-stilts on the Brunei River.

According to the poem, it was one of the brothers, Pateh Berbai, who got the idea of a "floating market, called *padian*, for selling all sorts of vegetables and commodities. He felt that since the population had grown large, a market on land could result in conflicts and disputes. But it is more convenient in boats on the water, with each *padian* (woman vendor) bringing her own commodities. Whenever there is a dispute, even with other tribes, it could be easily dispersed." This floating market was to be a prominent feature of life in the capital until just a few decades ago.

The poem also relates how some of the brothers happened to capture the daughter of the sultan of Johor and took her home to marry Awang Alak Betatar. The grieving Johor ruler sent a *burong pingai* (Bird of Life) — after which one of Kampong Ayer's wards is said to be named—in search of the princess. But she told the bird she was completely happy and asked it to tell her parents she was married to a descendant of the gods. This, plus the fame and glory of Brunei, persuaded the sultan to journey from Johor (rather than the other way around, as in the *Selasilah*). He converted the brothers to Islam, and oversaw the installation of Awang Alak Betatar as Sultan Muhammad and his brothers as holders of what were to become Brunei's traditional offices (many of their titles are still in use and were similar to those used in the sultanates of the Malay Peninsula).

Exotic Trade Items

While there was undoubtedly an important social connection with Johor, it was trade with other overseas powers—including China, Siam,

Malacca, India and Arabia — that made pagan Po-ni and Islamic Brunei go. Gold, diamonds, pepper and, above all, camphor, were among ancient Brunei's exports, but most of its other trade items no longer have the slightest appeal on world markets. There's simply not much demand these days for bezoar stones (solid deposits found in the guts of monkeys and porcupines, used for making medicinal potions) or anteater scales (used as magical charms).

Other valuable items collected from Borneo's great rain forests included beeswax, dammar (the sticky sap of certain trees that could be burned in lamps), the feathers of exotic birds, and *ketapang* fruit (its reddish extract — "dragon's blood" — was used for dyeing and tanning). The rain forests also yielded items that set the Chinese in particular sailing for their supposed powers as aphrodisiacs. The most important of these were rhinoceros horns, which were (and often still are) believed to be a powerful stimulant when ground into a powder and consumed. The sad result has been the decimation of Borneo's population of these creatures; only one pitifully small herd survives on Sabah's East Coast. Another magnificent creature that has been hunted onto the endangered species list is the helmeted hornbill, a bird which grows to about four feet in length. The solid, ivory-like protuberance above its beak was prized for carving into cups and jewelry. Also in high demand were the nests made by several species of cave-dwelling swifts with their own saliva — the ingredient in birds' nest soup that still makes it among the most expensive of delicacies. The nests are believed to contain health-promoting substances.

The existence of a strong connection with China is reflected in accounts of the second sultan, Ahmad, who is variously described as either Chinese or married to a Chinese woman. He had no sons to succeed him, so a son-in-law ascended to the throne. This was Sherif Ali, an Islamic religious leader said to have come from Taif in Persia and been a descendant of Amir-Muminin Hassan, a grandson of Prophet Muhammad. Sherif Ali spread the teachings of Islam among the people of Brunei under the first two sultans, and during his own reign, when he was known as Sultan Berkat (Blessed), he built the first mosque. He is the "Rajah Chermin" mentioned by Stamford Raffles as having tried to convert the Rajah of Majapahit. According to legend, he failed in his conversion attempt but nevertheless left the Javanese ruler convinced of his high eminence by transforming a basket of pomegranates, considered unfit as gifts for the Rajah, into precious stones.

Sultan Berkat is also credited with initiating the building of a great stone wall between the islands of Chermin and Keingaran at the mouth of the Brunei River. Its purpose was to narrow the entrance to the river, making it easier to keep enemy vessels from entering. The wall was created by sinking some 40 stone-laden junks between the two islands, with the work continuing through the reign of Sultan Berkat's son and successor, Sulaiman, and into that of the fifth sultan, Bolkiah.

Brunei's government was apparently evolving into the region's most centralized and well-ordered, for only in that way could it have organized and controlled trade in such a wide range of products from such an extensive area. The camphor, birds' nests and other produce went out of the great port of Brunei, and in came such things as brass armlets, beads, iron, glass, Chinese trade ceramics, and rolls of Indian and Bengal cloth. Also coming in was tribute — in the form of rice, gold, cloth, even slaves — from other territories which had not necessarily been conquered by Brunei, but recognized its power to do so if it wished.

By the end of the reign of Sultan Bolkiah, Brunei's empire was at its zenith; most if not all Borneo sultanates had been made vassal states, including Sambas, Kotaringin, Pontianak, Coti, Pasir, Tuli Tuli, Banjarmasin and Burau. Sultan Bolkiah was famed for his sea exploits, voyaging to Malacca and Java and conquering Sulu as well as briefly seizing Manila with the help of a cannon called *Si-Gantar Alam* (He Who Makes the Earth Shake). According to legend, Sultan Bolkiah once demonstrated the extent of his domain by taking a *gantang* (eight pounds) of pepper on a voyage and dropping a single peppercorn at each spot he landed until all were gone. He was also famous for playing a set of royal musical instruments — a drum and a lute — on ship, thereby earning the nickname *Nakhoda Ragam* (the Singing Captain). Sultan Bolkiah even died at sea, while returning from Java where he had just married a princess named Puteri Laila Menchanai. According to the *Selasilah*, the princess was not told of his death until their ship reached Brunei, whereupon she committed suicide in grief.

The various Borneo sultanates were headquartered at the mouths of rivers that led into the headhunting country of the interior tribes. It could hardly be said that the sultans ruled the inland animists or even all the coastal Muslims — rather, they controlled trade by controlling the river mouths. The tribespeople collected jungle produce — often having no idea why anyone would want, for example, a rhinoceros's horn or its toenails (these were used in medicines) — and bartered with traders for salt, cloth, ceramics, beads, and brass gongs and betelnut boxes. Many of these things came to be highly valued heirlooms and to function as the money of the interior.

Almost nothing is known of how the trade of ancient Brunei was organized, but during the 1800s it was observed that the sultans granted portions of the empire (then much diminished) to favored nobles and court officials to rule as they saw fit. They would collect fees from traders and often taxed villagers, and would pay the sultan annual tributes of fixed quantities of rice, sago, war boats, cotton, or gold.

Nor is much known about ancient Brunei's fighting forces. It is unlikely it had a large standing army or navy, but rather certain groups of men were called to arms in time of trouble. Muslim Kedayan and pagan Murut farmers probably made up a good portion of the land forces, while naval hands came from the Water City's large population of fishermen. Kampong Saba — one of the 30-plus wards of today's Kampong Ayer — has a long fishing and naval warfare tradition. It is closely associated with the Pengiran Temonggong, one of the four ministers of state and the naval commander in days gone by.

Magellan's Men

Different parts of the Water City seem to have taken on specialized functions early in Brunei's history. There were wards where members of the nobility lived with their followers, wards where particular crafts were practiced, others that were home to fishermen who used different kinds of nets, and wards that served as home base for adventurous seafaring traders. Specialization and a highly organized form of government probably had a lot to do with Brunei's predominance among the sultanates of the region, but these refinements were not obvious to the early European visitors.

Antonio Pigafetta provided the first European account of Brunei as chronicler of Magellan's Spanish fleet, which lost its leader during a skirmish with Cebu islanders in the Philippines and limped into Brunei Bay in 1521 with only two of its original five ships afloat. Pigafetta and his fellow sailors found the Muslim sultan's court to be the most impressive among all those encountered on their pioneering journey.

After anchoring in Brunei Bay, they were greeted by a group of elderly chiefs who arrived in a beautiful *perahu* (small boat), the bow and stern of which were worked in gold. Several days later eight of the visitors, including Pigafetta, were taken ashore for an audience with the sultan. A pair of silk-draped elephants (which are not native to Borneo) bore them first to the Shahbandar's (chief port official) house, where they spent the night, and next day to the magnificent palace surrounded by a brick wall mounted with cannons.

The sultan was waiting to receive them, seated chewing betel nut with one of his sons in an elevated room at the end of a great hall adorned with silk hangings. The hall was thronged with nobles and some 300 soldiers "with naked rapiers at their thighs." That the Water City was then a wealthy place indeed is indicated by Pigafetta's observation that "the men in the palace were all attired in cloth of gold and silk which covered their privies, and carried daggers with gold handles adorned with pearls and precious gems, and they had many rings on their hands."

As well, the Italian wrote, the sultan owned two perfectly round pearls as big as hen's eggs — or so he was told by some of the chiefs. This is particularly interesting in view of the Chinese description of Po-ni some 300 years earlier, where two huge pearls were said to be kept in a temple. According to one possible reconstruction of history, these same pearls were carried off by the Suluks in their attack of 1369. However, the Bruneis eventually brought Sulu back under their control and the pearls were recovered, to be boasted of to Pigafetta. Even to this day, pearls hold a special place in the Brunei mind, and many members of the nobility possess heirloom ancestral pearls.

Archaeological Finds

According to Pigafetta, the Brunei capital was built almost entirely over the water, with the houses made of wood and raised on tall pillars. However, the sultan's palace and the houses of certain high officials were built on land. It is widely accepted that the site was at Kota Batu, about four miles downriver from Bandar Seri Begawan. This conclusion is based not only on local tradition, but more strongly on archaeological excavations (led by the late former curator of the Sarawak Museum, Tom Harrison) that turned up various artifacts, as well as the only permanent buildings so far found in Borneo dating from pre–European times.

The finds confirmed long-standing trading links with the Asian mainland, and China in particular. Chinese ceramics were found dating from the Sung Dynasty (960–1368) and the succeeding Ming, and Sawankhalok ceramics from Siam dating from as early as the late 1200s were also found (also present were large amounts of soft earthenware which seemed to be of local manufacture).

Two kinds of coins were discovered as well: Chinese in the deeper soil layers, presumably indicating greater antiquity, and Brunei Islamic closer to the surface. Two of the Chinese coins were identified as from the T'ang Dynasty and dated at around 725, but most were dated later, up through about 1450. Pigafetta recorded that during his visit, the Bruneis were using Chinese bronze coins pierced in the middle so they could be strung, although most trade was carried out on a barter basis.

Of the tombstones found at Kota Batu, the earliest for which a date can be determined is 1432. What is believed to be the tomb of Sultan Bolkiah, who may have died just before or after the visit of Magellan's men, has in recent years been restored to become a minor tourist attraction.

Kota Batu translates as "Stone Fort," and indeed Pigafetta described the sultan's palace as being fronted by a large brick wall with towers in which were mounted 56 cannons of bronze and six of iron. The

Tomb of Brunei's fifth sultan, Bolkiah, who ruled in the early 1500s when the Brunei Empire was at its height (covering Borneo Island and much of the Philippines).

archaeological excavations revealed stone and marble that must have been brought from some distance away. There were walls of stone, and also upright squared hardwood posts which had been preserved (a rarity for wood items in the tropics) because they were below the water table.

Because wood normally decays rapidly in the tropics, we have to depend on written accounts to have any idea of what ancient Brunei houses and boats were like. According to Pigafetta, their ships were junks made of planks fastened with wooden pegs to just above the water line, above which the sides were of large bamboos. Bamboos also served as the masts, while the sails were of tree bark.

Their porcelain was said to be made of extremely white earth, which was left underground for 50 or so years as otherwise it would not be fine; fathers would therefore bury this white earth for their sons. It was believed that a dish made of this porcelain would break if poisoned food was put in it (it is still widely believed in Borneo that certain ceramic items have this same magical property). Pigafetta also noted that at high tide women would go in boats through the settlement selling goods (this was the *padian* market system said to have been established by Pateh Berbai).

Before the audience of Pigafetta and his companions with the sultan, an official told them they could not speak to the ruler directly. Rather, the official said, they should tell it to him "so that he could communicate it to one of higher rank. The latter would communicate it to a brother of the Governor, who was stationed in the smaller hall, and this man would communicate it by means of a speaking-tube through a hole in the wall to one who was inside with the King." The chief also taught them the proper way to greet the sultan, "making three obeisances to the King with our hands clasped over the head, raising first one foot and then kissing the hands towards him."

They told the sultan they represented the king of Spain, who asked only permission to trade in peace. The sultan replied "that since the King of Spain desired to be his friend, he was willing to be his." This atmosphere of friendship, however, was not to last long. Like most empires, Brunei's was based on trade — trade coveted by the emerging European sea powers that sailed into Asian waters in war fleets more powerful than any that could be launched by Brunei's sultan or the other rulers in the region.

The Portuguese

Malacca, often described as Southeast Asia's most important port although it may have been rivaled by Brunei, was seized by the Portuguese in 1511. This may have actually given a boost to Brunei as many merchants, especially Muslims, may have shifted their operations to the Borneo port. In subsequent years the Spanish, Dutch and English joined in the fight to become king of the region's trade hill, and all were to adversely affect Brunei's position.

The sultanate initially carried on a brisk trade with the Portuguese in Malacca, who were also the first of the Europeans to stake a claim to the Moluccas (known as the Spice Islands) on the opposite side of Borneo. Portuguese ships often called at Brunei when sailing between Malacca and the Moluccas. One of the earliest such ships arrived in 1526 with a Portuguese official bearing gifts for the sultan in order to cement ties of friendship and trade. Among the gifts was a tapestry depicting many men and women, including a life-size king seated on a throne with a crown on his head. The sultan had never seen such fabric and became suspicious, fearing that the woven king and his people would come alive in the middle of the night and kill him and seize his own throne. The agitated sultan ordered away the Portuguese, whom he suspected of being sorcerers, but in the end he accepted them after the tapestry was burned before his eyes. Within 10 years, however, relations between Brunei and Portugal became strained due to the harsh Portuguese treatment of the Muslims of the Moluccas.

Both Portugal and Brunei also cultivated trade relations with the various sultanates of the Malay Peninsula, including Pahang, where a bloody incident that affected all three parties happened in 1542. According to Portuguese merchants, they were robbed of their goods stored in warehouses by looters who went on a rampage after the Brunei sultan's ambassador killed the sultan of Pahang for committing adultery with his wife.

The Spanish

The Spanish followed hard on the heels of the Portuguese and made Manila their Southeast Asian base of operations. They soon began demanding that Brunei become a vassal state recognizing the authority of the Spanish king. The governor of the Philippines, Dr. Francisco de Sande, also demanded in 1576 that Brunei stop sending Islamic missionaries to Luzon as well as Sulu, which was still under the domination of Brunei.

However, Sultan Saiful Rijal (the seventh sultan and the first to be identified by name in European written sources) replied of course that there was no question of submitting to the Spanish king — and furthermore, Brunei would be expanding rather than stopping its missionary activities in Sulu while at the same time prohibiting Christian missionizing in its own territories.

According to the *Selasilah*, conflict and intrigue among top Brunei royalty contributed to the sultanate's ensuing brief subjugation by the Spanish. The key figures besides the sultan were the Pengiran Bendahara (probably the second most important official after the sultan) on the one hand and the Pengiran Seri Lela (the sultan's uncle) and the Pengiran Seri Ratna on the other. Things came to a head in the mid–1570s at the wedding of the latter's daughter and the former's son, when Pengiran Bendahara Sakam — a man famed for his bravery — brazenly kidnapped the bride and took her to his house. The aggrieved pengirans took the matter to the sultan, who agreed to punish Pengiran Bendahara Sakam.

However, the Pehin Orang Kaya Digadong also went to the sultan with a message from Pengiran Bendahara Sakam asking for forgiveness. He also explained the reason for his audacious act — to test the spirit of the people of Brunei. He stressed that if anyone tried to take what was theirs, *"Mereka yang berhak perlu berani berputeh tulang daripada berputeh mata"* (the owners must be so brave as to show their white bones — in other words, to die fighting — rather than the whites of their eyes). And the sultan handed down a pardon.

This decision so enraged the other two pengirans that, according to the *Selasilah*, they sneaked off to Manila and made a secret pact with the Spanish promising to help them defeat Brunei in exchange for the Pengiran Seri Lela being installed as sultan and the Pengiran Seri Ratna as Pengiran Bendahara.

Dr. de Sande himself led a fleet of some 40 boats which anchored near the mouth of the Brunei River in April 1578. He sent two Moro chiefs with copies of a letter to the sultan of Brunei and Mindanao (the largest island of Sulu) in which the demands to stop propagating Islam in the Philippines and to allow Christian missionaries into Brunei were repeated. The sultan's response was to order the chiefs killed (although one managed to escape) and his own warships to open fire on the Spanish. The enemy's artillery, however, proved to have a longer range and the Bruneis fled upriver where they abandoned their ships and dumped as many of the cannons as they could into the water. The pursuing Spanish seized 27 galleys and smaller ships and recovered 127 large and small cannons, according to a letter from Dr. de Sande to his king, Philip II. The Spanish also pillaged a large portion of the Water City's wealth.

The *Selasilah* says the main Brunei fort was breached due to the treachery of the Pengiran Seri Lela and the Pengiran Seri Ratna, and Sultan Saiful Rijal fled to Jerudong about 12 miles away. The annals go on to describe how Pengiran Bendahara Sakam took refuge on Ambok Island and began recruiting and training 1,000 warriors whom he led the following year to defeat and chase away the Spanish. For this the sultan named him heir-apparent.

This account is, however, at odds with what was recorded by the Spanish who were involved. In the above-mentioned letter to King Philip II, Dr. de Sande related that almost as soon as he'd won the military victory, all his soldiers fell ill (with cholera, it has been speculated) and he was forced to sail away in order to save them. However, some of the local chiefs (he named the Pengiran Maharaja Diraja and the Pengiran Seri Lela) had agreed to cooperate and meet the demands of the Spanish, and they were left to rule the sultanate.

Perhaps it was these traitorous pengirans, rather than the Spanish, whom Pengiran Bendahara Sakam defeated, for when Dr. de Sande sent a fleet back to Brunei in March 1579, Saiful Rijal was again back in control and his usurpers were either dead from disease or execution. This time the Spanish were under orders not to use force—not even to kill a cow for its meat—but to negotiate an alliance. Brunei, of course, would be very much the junior partner, required to make annual tribute of camphor, galleys or other products. But Sultan Saiful Rijal played a waiting game, failing to show up for meetings with the leader of the Spanish expedition. The sultan apparently felt he could withstand an attack this time around as he'd built a new fort further upriver where the Spanish ships with their big guns could not reach. In any case, they were under orders not to attack, and their frustrated leader finally decided to withdraw in fear of his men becoming sick from contaminated water, poor food, the effects of the rain and sun, and lack of exercise.

Another Venice

As a result of the Spanish habit of recording their activities in detail, we have descriptions of the Water City of that era which show it was as grand as when described by Pigafetta nearly 60 years earlier. According to one writer, "That city was very large and rich, and was built over a very broad and deep river and had the appearance of another Venice. The buildings were of wood, but the houses (on land) were excellently constructed of stone work and gilded, especially the king's palaces, which were of huge size. That city contained a very sumptuous mosque, a very large and interesting building, quite covered with half relief and gilded." The same writer described the city as "a staging post of great importance, for it is on the way from Malacca to the Moluccas and Manila, while it has an excellent harbor for the fleets which sail to Malacca destined for Patani, Siam and other kingdoms."

The invaders of 1578 found people from all over Southeast Asia — from the Moluccas, Mindanao, Java, Sumatra, Pahang, Patani, Siam, Cambodia, Cochin-China (present-day Vietnam) and China, among other places — showing just how important a port the Water City was. Extensive ties were especially evident between Brunei and Sulu, which was then ruled by a Brunei and was attacked by the Spanish at about the same time (this caused many Sulus to flee to Brunei).

It was also apparent that the organization of the sultanate's government and military were exceptionally complex for the region. There were jails and jailers, and in the sultan's palace were found letters from the Portuguese in Malacca, and one from the king of Portugal. The Portuguese were said to consider Brunei too powerful to try to conquer and contented themselves with minor trade by their ships plying between Malacca and the Moluccas.

The Dutch

Following the Portuguese and Spanish on to the scene were the Dutch. The first Dutchman to come a-trading was Admiral Olivier Van Oort, who arrived at the end of 1600 in search of pepper but left quickly as he suspected there was a plot to seize his ship. A trading relationship nevertheless did develop in the early 1600s, with some Dutch traders visiting Brunei and Brunei traders sailing to Batavia, the Dutch settlement on Java now known as Jakarta. The Dutch were also negotiating with various sultans elsewhere in Borneo, and one of their officials recorded how he was present at gold-rich Sambas on Borneo's west coast in 1610 and helped to fortify the town against an expected Brunei attack. Luckily for Sambas, rough seas forced the Brunei fleet to turn back.

At one point there was a strong possibility of a Dutch-Brunei military alliance against Spain, but nothing concrete came of this beyond a promise by the Dutch to come to Brunei's aid if it was again attacked by the Spanish. However, by the mid-1600s even this promise was dropped; the Dutch wanted to remain friends with Brunei but also hoped to develop trade with Manila. In the end, however, trade and diplomatic relations with both Brunei and Manila were to be virtually nonexistent. Brunei leaders seemed to distrust the Dutch — who after all were wooing subordinate sultans elsewhere in Borneo — and were later to consistently prefer dealing with the British above other Europeans.

Coins and Cannons

For a short period towards the end of the 1500s, the Spanish silver dollar replaced Chinese coins as the Brunei Empire's standard monetary unit. The first coins issued by Brunei itself may have appeared around this time, although the earliest so far identified came between 1600 and 1620 or so. This tin coin bore the title "Pengiran Bendahara" — at that time, Raja Dungu Muhammad, the brother of both the eighth sultan, Shah Berunai, and the ninth, Hassan (Sultan Adil, or The Just). The early Brunei coins reflected the strengthening of Islamic influence. Animals alien to Brunei, such as camels, were often depicted, suggesting the coins were designed by craftsmen from the Middle East. As well, honorific titles in Arabic were common, such as "Sultan Malik Al Dzahir" (The Acknowledged Ruler) and "Sultan Al Adil" (The Just Ruler).

Also around 1600 Brunei craftsmen apparently began casting brass cannons, which were to gain a reputation as among the best made in Southeast Asia. These served not only as weapons, but came to be valued as heirlooms among many of Borneo's native groups. At about this time, Chinese coins conveniently lost value due to the local minting of money, and many were melted down for use as a hardening agent in casting cannons and other brassware.

Sultan Hassan is believed to have been the last of the truly powerful rulers, after whom Brunei went into decline. He reasserted control over Sulu and established diplomatic ties with the sultanate of Acheh at the northern tip of Sumatra, which may have provided the administrative model which gave Sultan Hassan the idea of doubling the number of Brunei *wazir* (viziers, top court officials) from two to four. Previously there had been only the Pengiran Bendahara, who acted as the sultan's deputy and was in charge of land defense, and the Pengiran Temenggong, who was the naval chief and had various judicial functions as well. According to the *Selasilah*, Sultan Hassan added the Pengiran Digadong to take charge of both the treasury and palace affairs, and the Pengiran Pemancha to serve as the latter's assistant with special responsibility for ceremonial customs.

The system of government then was presumably similar to that observed by the British during the 1800s. The *wazirs* were all men of the royal family, as were the officials of the next lower rank, the *cheteria*. The most important of the *cheteria* was the Pengiran Shahbandar, who was akin to a "minister of commerce" in his capacity as chief port official. Below the *cheteria* were the *menteri*, who were appointed from among the non-noble classes and even from among non–Brunei Malays.

Distant Neighbors

The Portuguese were ousted from their Malacca foothold in 1641 by the Dutch, who also eventually took control of the Moluccas and the rest of modern-day Indonesia. The Spanish, however, continued to rule the Philippines (although never really gaining control of Muslim Sulu) until 1898 when, after their quick defeat in the Spanish-American War, they ceded the territory to the United States.

Following the Spanish attack on Brunei in 1578, contacts between the two powers over the ensuing centuries were few and far between. There were to be no further major military confrontations, although the Spanish did mount a small punitive expedition in 1649 against an outpost in Brunei-held northeastern Borneo (the present-day Malaysian state of Sabah). This was in retaliation for the activities of piratical "sea nomads" under Brunei's control. Within 40 years, however, the two sides were exchanging ambassadorial missions which established trade relations and ceded to Spain the island of Palawan, lying between Manila and the Borneo mainland.

The general lack of armed conflict between the Islamic sultanate and Roman Catholic Spain was probably due to two factors. One was that both were preoccupied with trying to hold their empires together in the face of intrusions by other European powers (and internal dissension, in Brunei's case). But more importantly, Sulu – the original source of conflict – gained its independence from Brunei and also successfully resisted Spanish subjugation. Marauding Sulu-based pirates severely hampered the sea trade of both Brunei and Spain, and Great Britain as well on its arrival later.

Civil War

Clear historical records of the era – and indeed right up until about 1850 – are lacking. The Spanish made references to Sulu having its own ruler as early as 1587, although Sultan Hassan was said to have reasserted control in the early 1600s. But it is certain that Sulu was independent by the 1660s, when Brunei was wracked by a civil war that undoubtedly contributed greatly to its decline.

According to the *Selasilah*, conflict began in 1661 when the son of the twelfth sultan, Muhammad Ali, killed a son of Pengiran Bendahara Abdul Momin, who took revenge by storming the palace with his men, executing the sultan and usurping the throne. There were an initial few years of relative peace, but the new Pengiran Bendahara, Muhyiddin, a nephew of the former sultan, was convinced to take revenge for his uncle's death.

Muhyiddin's secret supporters fomented trouble that led Sultan Abdul Momin to move to Pulau Chermin (Mirror Island) at the mouth of the Brunei River, where he felt safer. But this gave Muhyiddin, who stayed behind in the capital, the chance to declare himself the rightful heir to the throne and raise the yellow flag of the sultan, and the Bruneis split their allegiance between the two contenders. It was also at this time, according to some accounts, that Muhyiddin shifted the Water City from Kota Batu to a sharp bend about two miles upriver — the site of present-day Kampong Ayer. The move was apparently made for defensive reasons, as enemy ships coming upriver would have to sail into the fire of cannons mounted on riverside hills and then turn, exposing themselves to broadsides.

After some 12 years of conflict Abdul Momin was finally defeated. But before his defenses were overrun and he was killed, the *Selasilah* recounts, he defiantly ordered all inherited royal property destroyed — including the original bejeweled crown, which was stuffed into a cannon and shot into the South China Sea, where it presumably still rests.

There are differing accounts of the civil war, but all agree that Sulu sided with victorious Muhyiddin (who apparently commissioned the *Selasilah* to authenticate his claim to the throne). There is confusion, however, as to Sulu's reward — its independence, or if it had already gained this, control of the camphor-rich territories north of Brunei Bay that approximate present-day Sabah. The Brunei spirit was undimmed, however, if a Spanish visitor's account about 10 years after the end of the civil war can be taken as an indication. He wrote that numerous boats were always on the move from house to house, and the residents "continuously paddle about the river especially on moonlit nights to entertain themselves with their 'rabanas' (tambourines) and gongs, the only instruments used in their merrymaking."

Disintegration

Whatever the civil war's effect may have had on relations with Sulu, it is certain that the disintegration of the Brunei empire was well underway.

It is likely that the loss of Sulu was accompanied or soon followed by the freeing of other sultanates as vassal states, for the Dutch were well-established on the south and west coasts of Borneo by 1700.

The result must have been a sharp fall in trade through the Water City — and hence in Brunei's wealth and military might. Worse still, Sulu (which was never fully subdued by the Spanish) became an active opponent, vying for control of northeastern Borneo, which it claimed as its reward for helping Sultan Muhyiddin — a claim disputed by Brunei. At stake was not only territory but also followers, the most important being sea nomads who were needed for control of the crucial sea trading routes. The *Selasilah* relates how certain nomadic Bajau groups were considered the "property" of Brunei nobles and were transmitted by inheritance. But by the mid-1700s Brunei seems to have lost many if not most of its sea nomad followers, who turned to preying on the sultanate's own ships to such an extent that encouragement was given to the British to set up trading posts from which they would presumably help to control the pirates.

The initial British presence in the area came through the East India Company in Sulu territory. Alexander Dalrymple negotiated a concession for the company of the northern tip of the Borneo mainland and some offshore islands, of which he chose Balambangan for a base due to its two fine harbors. It was hoped that this location would attract Chinese trade away from the Dutch in Java and would also lure Bugis traders based on Borneo's east coast.

Dalrymple raised the British Union Jack over Balambangan at the start of 1763, but the trading post was not to be opened until eight years later. Shortly before Dalrymple was to sail from England to take charge of the post, he was dismissed from the company over a salary dispute and John Herbert was sent in his place. Herbert had had trading experience in the Malay Peninsula, but his lack of knowledge of Sulu ways resulted in bad feelings and a Suluk attack led by Dato Teting that drove the British out of Balambangan in 1775.

The Brunei sultan invited the retreating company men to accept the cession of the island of Labuan in Brunei Bay, or to set up shop on the mainland close to the Water City, which they accepted. The East India Company was also given a monopoly on Brunei's pepper trade. Most of the spice was grown by Chinese planters as far inland as the foot of mighty Mount Mulu (just over the border with present-day Sarawak) and traded with China. In return, the British were supposed to protect Brunei from Sulu piracy. The company, however, lost money on the venture and withdrew. In 1803 they again tried to set up a trading station on Balambangan and Brunei again offered Labuan, but within two years the company left the region once more. The time of the British would come only later that century.

One of the earliest British descriptions of Brunei appeared in Robert Forrest's account of his voyage to New Guinea and the Moluccas, which was published in 1779. As others had before him, he compared the Water City to Venice, with houses built over the water in orderly rows forming waterways. He estimated the Brunei River at that point to be about as wide as the Thames at London Bridge. Some of the houses were double-storied — the first such houses he'd seen over the water in the region — and some had raised walkways to make trading easy. Forrest also noted that four or five Chinese junks able to carry 500 to 600 tons each arrived from Amoy every year.

Brunei, however, was in serious economic decline. By 1800 the Water City's docks, capable of taking ships up to 600 tons, were no longer in use and most Chinese pepper planters had returned home. And by the 1830s Chinese junks stopped calling altogether. Certainly the coming of the Europeans was a major cause, as this disrupted long-established trade patterns and affected not only Brunei but all the many other trade-dependent sultanates of Southeast Asia. One of the biggest problems for the newcomers was sea piracy. Some historians see a good deal of irony in this, pointing out that European domination of trade led various local leaders to support — or at least turn a blind eye to — piracy as one of their few remaining sources of revenue. Some embittered rulers took the tack of severing relations with the Europeans. This was apparently the situation in Brunei during the early 1800s, as British Admiralty charts warned sailors it was "certain death to go up river to Brunei."

More Internal Strife

This was also a period when the sultanate was once again wracked by internal conflict over succession to the throne, following the death of Sultan Muhammad Tajuddin (the nineteenth sultan) in 1807. His 12-year reign is credited with putting a temporary halt to Brunei's decline, as he brought wayward district rulers back under control and sent envoys to Java and China. Sultan Tajuddin abdicated in 1806 in favor of a son who, however, only lived another six months, to be succeeded by Muhammad Kanzul 'Alam. He was to hold the throne for some 15 years, but because there were other claimants, he never had sufficient support to undergo the ritual coronation that would have made him Yang Dipertuan Brunei (He Who Is

Top: Part of present-day Kampong Ayer on the Brunei River — Bandar Seri Begawan is on the right bank; Arts and Handicrafts Center is under construction in the foreground. Bottom: Starting up the family boat in Kampong Ayer.

Made Ruler of Brunei). The real power was held by his son, a ruthless despot known as Raja Api (Fire King) because of his fiery temper.

Raja Api apparently lost a power struggle after his father's death in 1822, for he was executed a short while later. According to legend , he made a prophecy before his execution by strangulation — if his body fell on its right side, Brunei would enjoy good times, but if on the left side, they would be bad. His body fell left, and peace and prosperity did continue to elude Brunei. The elimination of Raja Api was followed by a change of policy towards the British, for a trade mission was then sent to the recently founded port of Singapore, mainly to seek buyers for antimony which had been found in the district of Sarawak at the sultanate's western end.

Sultan Omar Ali Saifuddin II succeeded to the throne, but he was never coronated as Yang Dipertuan either, because of opposition from some of the nobility. According to Brunei ideals, the sultan ruled with the consent of his fellow nobles. He was to be chosen from the small pool of eligible males of the royal family, and must never rule oppressively. Rather, all important decisions were to be made after consultation with councils of nobles and advisors. During the 1800s the British noted that agreements signed by the sultan also required the seals of at least two other high officials, the most important of these being the four ministers of state (Pengiran Bendahara, Pengiran Digadong, Pengiran Temenggong and Pengiran Pemancha).

Succession problems were most likely to arise when a sultan died without leaving a son of sufficient age. Then his brothers, half-brothers, uncles and nephews might start scheming with an eye to the throne. Tension was such in the mid–1800s that one visitor reported four of the Water City's wards had loaded their cannons and aimed them at each other. This incident underlines the fact that nobles of high standing lived in particular wards with their followers. In the best of times they would unite behind the sultan — but in the worst, as during much of the 1800s, some of them might openly oppose him.

II

Turning to the British

Internal strife probably had a lot to do with Brunei's nineteenth century loss of control over much of its remaining territory extending down Borneo's northwest coast – a situation that made possible the remarkable saga of James Brooke, who was to serve as the model for Joseph Conrad's Lord Jim. When the English adventurer arrived on the scene in 1839 – with high hopes of making his fortune, buttressing the British presence in Southeast Asia and introducing "civilization" – there was a rebellion under-way in the district of Sarawak (Brunei's remotest remaining possession, about 600 miles southwest of the Water City). This came in response to the oppressive rule of Pengiran Indera Mahkota, the district's governor. He forced many native Land Dayaks to work in the antimony mines at low pay, and also made the local Malays his enemies by his economic monopoly which threatened their trade-derived prosperity. When the Land Dayaks began to rebel in 1835, the Malays stepped in as leaders.

Palace intrigue also contributed to the revolt. The chief players were Pengiran Usop (father-in-law of the sultan's son) and the Pengiran Bendahara, Muda Hashim, who was a brother of the hated Raja Api yet of quite a different character, with a reputation among Europeans as "humane and progressive." Pengiran Usop, however, resented Pengiran Muda Hashim's position as Bendahara, and he and his allies contrived to have Pengiran Muda Hashim and his brother sent to Sarawak – in effect, exiled, for it gave Pengiran Usop the chance to take over as Bendahara. He also tried to make his rival look bad by secretly encouraging the rebels to obtain support from the sultan of Sambas (a former Brunei vassal state on Borneo's west coast) and the Dutch assistant resident there. Pengiran Indera Mahkota was also as obstructive as possible.

Muda Hashim couldn't put down the rebellion until Brooke helped him with a force of local natives he raised and led. The Englishman's reward was to be made governor of Sarawak by Muda Hashim under an agreement signed in September 1841. And in July the following year he was annointed Sarawak's Rajah – the "White Rajah" – by the twenty-third sultan, Omar

Ali Saifuddin II. The sultan's hope was apparently that through Brooke, Brunei would be granted the British protection which had been sought as early as the 1770s. In the meantime, Brooke was considered an official of the sultan who, in the traditional way, was given rule over a territory in exchange for a large portion of annual revenues. But the Englishman had bigger ideas, and once he gained a foothold in Borneo he proceeded to gobble up huge chunks of Brunei territory.

The British Are Coming

Muda Hashim, in turn, needed Brooke and his aura of being British-backed (in fact he wasn't, as yet), for although the pengiran was next in line for the throne (the sultan lacked a legitimate son), he and his family could not stand up to their opponents in the Water City. He only dared to return to the capital with a British naval force in 1844 when he was restored as Bendahara largely as a result of Brooke's support, based on the belief that here was a Bruneian who sincerely wanted to cooperate in opening up trade and suppressing piracy. Hopes on this score were expressed in black and white in 1843 when Brooke accompanied Captain Sir Edward Belcher to the Water City, where a preliminary treaty with the British was signed (and Brooke took the opportunity to gain the right to bequeath Sarawak to his heirs). The sultan, hoping for an eventual treaty of protection, agreed to open up trade, avoid non–British alliances and work to suppress piracy.

The White Rajah's strategy for gaining a fiefdom of his own was to win British recognition. One step in this direction, he knew, was to "civilize" the area under his control by putting a stop to headhunting and piracy. He accomplished this by recruiting native groups as allies (who, ironically, often took enemy heads on Brooke-organized punitive expeditions against recalcitrant headhunters) and also gaining the help of British naval officers whose ships were used to smash pirate strongholds. In 1843, for example, Captain Henry Keppel's *Dido* was used to wipe out a pirate base on the Saribas River on the Brunei side of the Sarawak District—for Brooke claimed the right to operate outside his little territory against those who posed a threat to its security.

Pengiran Usop, naturally, was strongly anti–Brooke and, by extension, anti–British. He was known to be allied with Sherif Usman, a pirate leader who controlled Marudu Bay at Borneo's northern tip, and who is remembered to this day by the people of the area for his brutal, oppressive ways. Sherif Usman (those who called themselves "Sherif" were Arabs claiming descent from Prophet Muhammad) threatened to attack Sarawak, earning a preemptive British naval strike. He escaped but was later executed on the sultan's order. Brooke pressure also led the sultan to agree to the execution of Pengiran Usop, who after all had been in league with an ally of the enemy Sulu (Sherif Usman). For the British, his greatest sin was to have been deeply involved in the slave trade.

The sultan continued to see the British as potential saviors. The famous American warship *Constitution* called in 1845 with an offer of a treaty of protection and trade in exchange for exclusive rights to coal at Muara near the Water City. But Brunei rejected the American offer as it was awaiting a reply from the British on a similar proposal that would give them Labuan Island (they were weighing this against a return to Sulu-held Balambangan). In 1850, however, the United States did sign a commercial treaty with Brunei.

In the meantime, the power struggle continued in the capital. Muda Hashim's reinstallment as bendahara apparently made his family arrogant and he had little support except among the traders who saw profits in dealing with the British. Then in early 1846 he and about a dozen of his close relatives went the way of Pengiran Usop when they were massacred by men led by Pengiran Anak Hashim (the sultan's illegitimate son with designs on the throne) and Haji Saman — and the sultan himself was probably in on the plot as well. An enraged Brooke took the affair as a personal insult and convinced Admiral Sir Thomas Cochrane to send a seven-ship Royal Navy fleet up the Brunei River. In fact, the Admiral had no intention of attacking the Water City, as such buccaneering activities had been forbidden following British Parliamentary inquiries into various bloody naval affairs, including several mounted on Brooke's behalf (against "pirates" or "political opponents," depending on one's point of view).

The Bruneis expected an attack and had put up bamboo barriers in the river and stuck logs in the riverbed, which barely slowed the British ships. Haji Saman, commanding one of several riverside forts, opened fire with cannons, and the warships returned it. It was a brief, unequal battle in which the British seized many Brunei-made brass cannons (which were later melted down and recast for use in the Crimean War). The sultan and top officials took refuge at Damuan about 15 miles away but soon abandoned their fort to be razed by the pursuing British and fled into the jungle. Cochrane and Brooke withdrew, leaving Captain Rodney Mundy to settle things with the sultan, who undoubtedly felt there was no choice but to promise to stick with the British.

Haji Saman, on the other hand, vowed to fight on and built a fort on the Membakut River not far away in present-day Sabah. But Captain Mundy destroyed the fort and forced the local natives to stop supporting the renegade by threatening to destroy their rice crops. Haji Saman surrendered himself the following year to the sultan, but the British pardoned him on condition he caused no more trouble — and to this day he is remembered in Brunei as something of a hero for standing up to the foreign power.

In December 1846, Britain and Brunei finally signed an agreement ceding Labuan, with both parties agreeing to cooperate in suppressing piracy. This was followed up by the 1847 Treaty of Friendship and Commerce, which confirmed the joint anti-piracy stand, established the position of consul-general for Borneo (Brooke was the first, as well as governor of Labuan), and made it necessary for the sultan to get British consent to transfer any territory (transfers were nevertheless to be freely made). For Brunei, the treaty held the false hope that British protection was at hand.

Mid-Nineteenth Century Brunei

The growth of close relations brought Englishmen and other Europeans to Brunei who were fascinated by the Water City and recorded their observations in words and paintings. These give us our earliest detailed (though perhaps often biased) look at life over the water.

There was, for example, Frank Maryatt's *Brunei and the East Indian Archipelago*, published in 1848, which described the *padian* market:

> The greatest novelty at Brunei is the floating bazaar. There are no shops in the city, and the market is held every day in canoes. These come at sunrise every morning from every part of the river, laden with fresh fruit, tobacco, pepper and every other article which is produced in the vicinity; a few European productions, such as handkerchiefs, check-cotton prints, etc., also make their appearance. Congregated on the "main street" the canoes are tacked together, forming lanes through which the purchasers in their own canoes, paddle, selecting and bargaining for their goods with as much convenience as if the whole was transacted on *terra firma*. Iron is here so valuable that it is used as money. One hundred flat pieces an inch square are valued at a dollar, and among the lower classes these iron pieces form the sole coin. They are unstamped, so that every person appears at liberty to cut his own iron into money; but whether such is really the case I cannot vouch.

The *padian* peddlers were all women, who were apparently of the slave or lower classes as women of higher rank would not have been allowed to move about freely on their own.

The most detailed and, apparently, reliable account was written by Spenser St. John, who lived in the Kota Batu area after succeeding Brooke as consul-general. St. John listed the Water City's wards and the main occupations in each, which were often reflected in ward names. Thus Pabalat was the home of fishermen who planted *pabalat* nets on poles in the sand and mud banks of the bay and river; and Perambat of those who used fine-mesh *rambat* (casting nets) to catch prawns and small fish (both wards are now part of Kampong Saba). The residents of another ward specialized in cleaning rice and making rice mortars, the women of another

Selling prawns and fish at a riverside dock in Bandar Seri Begawan.

in threading together *nipah* palm leaf roofing mats. Burong Pingai (as it is still known) was the home of wealthy traders who dealt in jungle produce from other parts of Borneo. Woodworkers, brassware-makers, blacksmiths, goldsmiths — all tended to be grouped together in certain wards, with most of the nobility and higher-ranking government officials living in the center of the Water City's northern section, on either side of the Kedayan River's mouth.

St. John also noted that the sultan was widely regarded as endowed with certain magical powers. He owned for example a sacred *gusi* jar, and the natives would come and give him presents in return for "a little water from this sacred jar, with which to besprinkle their field to ensure good crops."

A Compromise Sultan

When Sultan Omar Ali Saifuddin II died in 1852 without leaving a son born of a noble wife, open conflict threatened to erupt as two factions promoted their own choices as his successor. One was Pengiran Anak Hashim, the late sultan's son by a concubine and still a young man, and the other was Pengiran Muda Muhammad, brother of murdered Brooke favorite Pengiran Muda Hashim. But Brooke wielded his influence (which had grown considerably after the British appointed him to represent them in Borneo) to bring about the compromise selection of Pengiran Abdul Mumin, who had been bendahara. The competing factions were mollified by giving them the various vizier posts. Pengiran Indera Mahkota, who had strongly opposed Brooke's taking over his Sarawak governorship, was made Pengiran Shahbandar. According to a story still told in Brunei, in 1858 Brooke got members of the late Pengiran Muda Hashim's family to convince Pengiran Indera Mahkota there was trouble in Limbang and he should lead a force there. On the way, his boat capsized in mysterious circumstances and he drowned as he couldn't swim.

Brooke's part in helping to restore unity among the nobility in 1852 raised his prestige in Brunei and allowed him to negotiate the cession of seven contiguous river districts, the first of what were to be additions to his toehold in Sarawak. Chunk by chunk, Sarawak grew and Brunei shrank — each transfer of territory in exchange for an annual fee that was apparently much needed by the sultan, who had few other remaining sources of revenue.

However, concern was voiced in Britain about the way the White Rajah and his nephew Charles Brooke — who was to become the second White Rajah — were building their own private fiefdom. There were questions about their recruitment of headhunters to subdue rebellious tribes, and concern over the dismemberment of Brunei. The Brookes replied that Sarawak's expansion served to put a stop to headhunting, piracy, slavery and oppressive district rulers who'd slipped out of the Brunei sultan's control.

While some Brunei nobles and officials profited from connections with the Brookes and the British, many others wanted a return to the situation in which their rule was supreme. One thing they disliked was that escaped slaves were given sanctuary at the nearby Colony of Labuan, the governor of which, G.W. Edwards, managed to temporarily patch up differences on the issue in 1857.

A major impact of Labuan on Brunei came as the result of British encouragement to Chinese traders to set up shop on the island. The British had found the energetic and commercially oriented Chinese to excel at developing the economies of Singapore and various Malayan towns with minimal government assistance, and hoped they would do the same for Labuan. As the Chinese became established there, various Brunei nobles also came to appreciate their commercial skills and recruited them as tax collectors or to run trade monopolies. Chinese traders also went into business in the Water City, displacing Brunei Malay traders of long standing. By the end of the century, most businesses were in Chinese hands – a situation that has prevailed to the present.

Intrigue among the nobility was never-ending. The sultan appointed Pengiran Dipa as chief of Mukah, a district along the coast between Sarawak and Brunei. His family was murdered in the 1850s by Pengiran Matusin, who was given sanctuary in Sarawak. Mukah was then taken over by Sherif Masahor, whom the Brookes blamed for the murder of two of their officers and who cut off trade with Sarawak. The Brookes tried gunboat diplomacy in 1860 but the sherif refused to open the Mukah River to trade, and a naval battle was in progress when Edwards arrived in a steamer and put a stop to it. For this he was dismissed as governor of Labuan because the British Foreign Office disapproved of his interference without having been invited by either side.

In the end, James Brooke achieved his goal in 1863 when he and St. John arranged to relieve the sultan of "further trouble" through the cession for a hefty annual sum of Mukah and Bintulu – the "Sago Rivers" along which sago palms flourished, providing a major source of export earnings for Sarawak well into the twentieth century. The sultan signed not only for the money, but also on seeing that St. John, the trusted British point man in Borneo, supported the Brooke plan.

North Borneo

Brunei also proved to be vulnerable to the northeast, where its claim was disputed by Sulu. Brunei had effective control over only parts of the territory's west coast, while Sulu controlled parts of the east – and many parts were virtual no-man's-lands where slavers and pirates operated without giving allegiance to anyone.

In 1865, the United States revived the dormant commercial treaty with Brunei signed 15 years earlier, posting C. L. Moses as consul. Moses was given a 10-year concession for northern Borneo in exchange for annual payments to both the sultan and the Pengiran Temenggong. The advantage for the Brunei side was not entirely monetary, for it was felt that a counterweight to expansionist Sarawak would be established.

Charles Brooke, who was soon to succeed his uncle as White Rajah, meanwhile tried to obtain the Baram, a large river only about 85 miles to the southeast of the Brunei capital. But the sultan refused to agree to the deal in 1868, describing the Baram as "the well from which our people drink water" (it was actually most valuable as the home of the much-feared Kayans, who sometimes fought on Brunei's behalf).

Moses sold his rights to another American whose trading company failed to make a go of it, but whose activities at least made the British take notice and start paying more attention to what was happening in Borneo. They asked the American government about its intentions and were assured it had no political ambitions in the area, and they also forbade any further territorial changes for 10 years. One consideration was that the Spanish and Germans were showing an interest and the British wanted to prevent them from making any deals with Brunei. And to further solidify the British presence, a royal charter (providing a measure of protection) was granted to a British business group which had obtained the previously American-held rights to northern Borneo (they also took the precaution of making a separate cession agreement with the sultan of Sulu, who claimed much of the same area).

The granting of the charter brought a protest from the Dutch, who pointed to the 1824 Anglo-Dutch treaty in which Britain agreed to stay out of the islands of the East Indies south of the equator. However, the equator bisects Borneo Island, with the territory obtained by the British North Borneo Chartered Company lying even further north than Brunei and Sarawak. The Dutch finally agreed that the treaty did not apply to the northern part of Borneo. The island's partition into two distinct areas, British and Dutch Borneo, became that much more of a fact accepted by the international community.

In early 1880, Commander Schufeldt of the United States Navy lodged a protest with the Brunei sultan over the cession of territory to the British North Borneo Chartered Company, on the basis of the 1850 Brunei–United States commercial treaty. The sultan's rebuttal included the points that he was an independent sovereign, that no agreement not to cede territory had been made with the United States, and that the United States had made no objections when northern Borneo territory had been ceded to its own citizens in the mid–1860s. And that pretty much ended official United States interest in Brunei until after World War II.

One significant consequence of the granting of the charter was that the British government decided to lift the ban on Sarawak expansion out of "fairness." The Kayans had in any case rebelled in the meantime, starting in 1874, over oppression and high taxes, and the sultan finally agreed to let Rajah Brooke have the troubled Baram River area plus all the other territory down to Bintulu.

As might be expected, matters of territorial lease or transfer often involved palace intrigue. In 1884, the British North Borneo Chartered Company sought to extend its territory further towards the Brunei capital by obtaining the Padas River. A deal was made with Sultan Abdul Mumin, but the chief owner, Pengiran Anak Hashim, who had been made Pengiran Temenggong, refused to affix his seal. That same year, the Temenggong gave the Trusan and Limbang rivers to Sarawak but the cession did not take effect because the sultan withheld his approval. With various nobles apparently rushing to sell their land, and the Germans or even the French in a position to possibly seize Brunei, the British Colonial Office recommended that the remainder of the shrunken sultanate be divided between Sarawak and the North Borneo Company. Fortunately for Brunei, a mission was sent to study the situation first. Sultan Abdul Mumin also took action in 1885 by calling all the pengirans to take an *amanah* (oath) not to alienate any more land.

The Loss of Limbang

The pengirans were for the most part to uphold their oath (they didn't have much land left in any case), but Brunei was still to lose its most populous and richest food-growing district, Limbang. Pengiran Anak Hashim himself was largely responsible by imposing oppressive taxes which led to the murder of two of his tax collectors in 1884 and the start of a revolt. When he became sultan the following year on Abdul Mumin's death, most of the people of Limbang refused to pay homage.

All of this gave Charles Brooke the chance to pry away another part of Brunei. He in fact wanted the entire sultanate, which he and his uncle had always considered an obstacle to progress and prosperity according to the British ideal. However, the Weld Mission visited Brunei and came away believing that the ancient sultanate was worth preserving, the sultan having stated that he could not believe the queen would give away his country without his consent. The Mission recommended that Brunei be made a full British protectorate with a resident (the British Residency system had already been introduced in various sultanates of the Malay Peninsula, with the resident taking over administration of the government and the sultan remaining as figurehead ruler with control only over Islamic religious matters).

The idea of introducing a resident in Brunei was, however, rejected because the sultan was as yet unwilling to yield so much power, and more importantly because there was no money to pay for it. But on September 17, 1888, Brunei became a protectorate, retaining internal independence but with the British responsible for foreign relations. Sarawak and North Borneo also became protectorates, the British thus securing the entire northern flank of Borneo.

It was then a rude shock to Brunei to lose Limbang two years later when Charles Brooke seized it on the basis that the chiefs there preferred Sarawak rule. It was also claimed that Pengiran Muda Bendahara, the district's principal owner, wanted to cede it. Sultan Hashim and his pengirans appealed to London, and the new British consul to Borneo, Noel P. Trevener, was told to file a report. The crucial issue, according to London, was whether Limbang had been "independent" prior to seizure — and Trevener said it had been since the revolt there began six years earlier. He reported that 12 of 15 headmen preferred Sarawak, although the sultan contended that Trevener had been drunk when he met the headmen and the vote was actually the other way around. Based on Trevener's report, the authorities in London approved Sarawak's move without being aware that the excision of Limbang divided Brunei into two, with the small Temburong District left dangling by itself. By the time they realized how odd this made the map look, they felt it was too late to reverse their decision.

The Singapore-based High Commissioner for Borneo, Sir Clementi Smith, thought he solved the dispute by recommending that Rajah Brooke offer the sultan a reasonable sum for Limbang. If it was refused, it would be deposited for future collection, to be returned to Sarawak after a certain period. The reasoning was that the sultan and his nobles were so much in need of cash that they would be forced to accept the offer. Yet Sultan Hashim remained adamant, earning considerable respect for sticking to his principles, and the money was returned to Sarawak in 1895. Sympathetic British officials spoke on Brunei's behalf in ensuing years, but as far as the Foreign Office was concerned, the case was closed. The loss of Limbang has not been fully accepted in Brunei to this day.

Other Revolts

The transfer of Limbang induced similar dreams among subject peoples very close to the Brunei capital, and there were serious revolts in both Tutong and Belait in 1899. Exploitation was again the root cause, and several chiefs from both districts had petitioned to join Sarawak four years earlier. Illustrative of the actions of Brunei nobles was the collection of three years' taxes in advance along the Belait River by the Pengiran Bendahara, who then offered to sell the district to Sarawak. This could not be done, however, as the sultan refused his consent. The 1899 revolt in Belait began when five of the bendahara's men were murdered as they collected "contributions" from villagers for a wedding of some of his relatives. In Tutong, the revolt resulted from oppression by the Pengiran Digadong.

The White Rajah hopefully telegrammed the Foreign Office saying that the rebellious districts should be annexed by Sarawak, but was told to wait. He also offered hefty monthly payments to the sultan, the bendahara and the pemancha, and their descendants, to take over the entire sultanate. Hashim absolutely rejected the idea, saying, "What would happen to me, my chiefs and my descendants? I should be like a tree stripped of branches and twigs."

The sultan also pressed his case everywhere he could, gaining the support of the governor of North Borneo (who was of course against expansion by his Sarawak rivals), catching the attention of King Edward VII, and obtaining publicity in newspapers from Singapore to London. This public relations campaign—and especially hints that Brunei might turn to the United States or Turkey—prompted the British to finally commit themselves to the preservation of Brunei. The sultan, however, would have to sacrifice Brunei's independence and accept a British resident.

Tough negotiations led to the signing of a treaty on December 3, 1906. It made Brunei a "full" protectorate, assured the succession of the ruling dynasty, introduced a resident, and provided for yearly allowances for the sultan, the bendahara and the pemancha (the only two viziers in office), with all the trade monopolies and rights of taxation held by various nobles to be redeemed. The State Council was formalized as the supreme law-making body, with the sultan as president, plus two viziers, two *cheteria*, three *menteri*, the resident and the assistant resident. In practice, however, the resident's word was law.

Because of the sultanate's impoverishment, money had to be borrowed from the Federated Malay States to finance the introduction of the residency system. The main expense was the redemption of the various tax rights and trade monopolies which the sultan had granted either on a particular item, such as rice, or in certain areas. Due to lack of funds, the governor of Labuan also served as the Brunei resident until 1915, when separate posts were introduced.

"Wreck of Past Glory"

Along with the sultanate's economy, the Water City had also suffered serious decline. Its population had shrunk to roughly 10,000, compared to perhaps twice that number around 1850, and its physical condition was such that it was described as "the miserable wreck of past glory" by Hugh Clifford, writing about a visit to Brunei for *Macmillan's Magazine* in 1902.

Clifford's description of the view on approaching the mouth of the Brunei River in a "little steam-yacht" is still apt: "Behind us, seemingly afloat upon the quiet sea, lay little islands smothered in foliage to the water's edge; before us the mainland of Borneo rose in a tumble of low hills, grass-grown or spattered with secondary scrub, with line upon line of faint blue mountains set against the paleness of a white-hot sky."

About 10 miles upriver they passed a bend — "and the town of Brunei lay sprawling upon the surface of the stream," overhung by "a thick haze, the smoke of many cooking-fires." The city was a "maze of narrow waterways hedged about only by the *nibong* piles, set apart at irregular intervals, upon which the crazy verandahs and huts tottered uneasily. In each of these lanes boats rode moored to ladders by rattan painters; on either hand rose buildings fashioned of wood, bark, or palm-leaf, inexpressably squalid, dirty, irregular, and picturesque."

Was this, Clifford wondered, really the place that was once "so imposing and magnificent" that it never failed to fill visitors "with awe and wonder?" The palace of the near-bankrupt sultan was distinguished from the Water City's other structures by little more than its greater size, having typically frail (to European eyes) wooden landing stairs leading up from the water and walkways of split palm trunks. It did, however, have a roof of patched corrugated iron instead of palm thatch. On a visit to the palace for an audience with Sultan Hashim — who appeared in "a flowing coat of white embroidered with tiny gold stars" — Clifford noticed that "brass swivel-guns grinned at us from unexpected corners." These were fired in customary salute to the visitors.

A more detailed sketch of the period's capital is found in Peter Blundell's *The City of Many Waters* — a book which, despite its title, is mostly about the author's personal life and work as an engineer at one of Brunei's very few industrial enterprises during the early part of the century. This was a riverside factory that processed mangrove tree bark into cutch, once an essential ingredient for tanning leather; it was also used for dyeing cloth khaki color.

Blundell's introduction to life in the Water City came as his boat steamed up the Brunei River and encountered canoes. "Presently one passes us, rushing upriver on the tide with the speed of a racing eight. A mass of brown fishing net protruded from its bow, half a dozen paddlers naked to the waist labored at the clanking paddles, a steersman sat perched on the curved stern. They were fishermen going home with the day's catch." The newcomer was to learn that although Brunei had declined in many respects, the bay and river remained rich in seafood that was a staple part of the diet. It was harvested with a bewildering variety of traps, nets, pots and hook-and-line combinations.

During visits to the Water City from his bungalow on land, Blundell discovered — as had Spenser St. John — that each ward tended to specialize in just one or two occupations. The Kedayan River area was (and still is) home to most of the craftsmen. Also living there were money-lenders, who provided an important service in those bankless days. In contrast to present-day Kampong Ayer, there were few walkways and most people paddled from place to place.

Blundell provides vivid descriptions of some of the craftsmen:

> You must risk a fall in the mud if you wish to see the Brunei silversmith at work. The sight is worth the risk. His workshop is a small hut with reed walls and split-palm floor covered with matting. He squats on the matting, usually exhibiting a pair of large feet and thin brown legs. The implements of his craft surround him. These consist of the silver, the resin, the hammer, the punches and various wooden blocks. He beats the silver into the required shape, then takes his mixture of hot resin and other ingredients and runs it around the article. This prevents any buckling while the pattern is being put on with punches. Putting on the pattern requires much thought, patience, and labor.

By contrast, the brass-founders on the Kedayan River's fringe "were rough of voice and fierce of demeanor." Their "foundries were built over the water. I remember their spaciousness and the excellence of the fire-clay that was used in them — it is plentiful in the valleys of the country round. I remember the moulds, dollies and queer-shaped wooden tools the founders used, the furnaces built of native bricks and clay, the charcoal, and, most vividly of all, the ingenious bellows constructed out of the hollow trunks of trees."

Blundell also noted that krises (the wavy-edged Malay dagger) and war swords were no longer in great demand, but were still made and often given an antique look by covering them "with what looks like old blood stains. For are there not many wealthy and ignorant persons touring the East?"

A Resident and a Regency

The end of Blundell's narrative was marked by the arrival of the first resident, Stewart McArthur (the chief British negotiator for the Residency treaty), shortly before the death of Sultan Hashim. The sultan had been very concerned that the treaty guarantee the succession of the dynasty. He designated his son Muhammad Jamalul Alam II as his successor, but he was under age so a regency was established. Once again, palace intrigue came into play as the bendahara opposed the residency idea and still wanted to sell Brunei to Sarawak, while the White Rajah backed the bendahara for the throne. According to Brunei tradition, the bendahara should have been regent until the new sultan came of age, but in this case a joint regency with the pemancha was named.

The bendahara, however, influenced the young sultan to send a petition signed by a number of pengirans asking the British to reverse various reforms being introduced by the resident. But the sultan soon learned who was really in charge and ended his opposition after the British reduced his stipend and threatened to depose him.

The residents gradually introduced a Western-style civil service. Customs, postal, agricultural, public works, and judicial departments were set up, followed later by police, medical and education. There were five districts administered by Malay officers, while local chiefs and village heads were appointed with functions like those of "officers of the peace."

One of the trickiest tasks of the residents was buying over the various trade monopolies, tax rights and cession monies, in order to gain revenue sources for the new-style government. Some pengirans tried to take advantage of the situation by artificially inflating their claims; some, including the sultan himself, forged the seal of the former ruler and affixed it to fictitious documents granting them various rights. Nevertheless, the redemption process was completed by 1914 except for a monopoly held by the rajah of Sarawak at Muara Damit, which was obtained in 1924.

Another move aimed at creating a revenue base was a land code introduced in 1909 and providing for titles, with land not under title considered state land. This, however, was intensely opposed by native groups, particularly the Kedayans concentrated in the area of the capital, who had a tradition of hereditary rights with whoever first cleared a piece of land and his descendants considered the owners. This problem was resolved by the setting aside of what were called "Kedayan Reserves." This still left large tracts under state control, some of which were opened up by European rubber planters or leased out for exploration by oil companies.

By 1911, Brunei was able to pay its own way. Cutch accounted for more than 90 percent of the value of its exports, followed by coal — mined at Brooketon (now Muara) — jungle produce, sago, and brass and silver products. Jungle produce exports were, of course, no longer on the huge scale of previous centuries and consisted mainly of rattan, dammar and, above all, the rubbery latex — known as jelutong — of wild-growing trees. Camphor was no longer important as it came mainly from territories which Brunei had lost.

From Water to Land

The British residents made a significant impact on today's capital through their efforts to direct the Water City's expansion to adjacent land. Sultan Muhammad Jamalul Alam II moved to a new palace on land in 1909, and a year later the Chinese shopkeepers began coming ashore.

Several of the early residents believed it would be better to resettle everyone on solid earth, arguing that life over the water was unhealthy. They felt that the women and children lacked exercise because they were always cooped up in their houses (there were few walkways in those days), and this made them more susceptible to diseases. These included cholera and dysentery, and filthy river water was blamed for the epidemics that periodically swept the water community. And, it was noted, many children had fallen into the river and drowned. But except for one group of water villagers that shifted to Temasik in 1909, the government had little success in its resettlement efforts.

Wrote acting resident B. O. Stoney in the 1909 Brunei Annual Report: "Though they admitted that they would be better off on the land, where they could cultivate small holdings and rear live-stock and poultry, yet they feared to snap the chains of custom which bound them to their semi-amphibious life. The women proved the greatest stumbling block. Many of the men said that they would move if only their wives would allow them to do so."

Serious thought was given to forced resettlement, but the idea was eventually abandoned. The change of view was expressed by the resident, G.E. Cators, in the Annual Report for 1918. Noting that the only real health problem that year was an influenza epidemic that hit the recently established rubber estates but bypassed the water community, he said: "Much has been written of the unhealthiness of Brunei houses perched as they are on mudbanks: but after this year's experience it may be doubted whether the system is altogether bad. The drainage is certainly better than that of a Malay kampong and the houses are fully exposed to the cleansing influence of sun, wind and rain."

Also described in that annual report was the coronation of Sultan Muhammad, 12 years after he'd taken the throne: "The scene as, to the roll of royal drums, the Pengiran Bendahara called in the ancient formula on the Sultan's subjects 'who are as the dew upon the earth and as the drops of the sea' to do obeisance was picturesque and impressive and no-one could fail to be moved by the passion of loyalty evoked." Sultan Muhammad was to die six years later, apparently of malaria, at the age of 38; Ahmad Tajuddin was his successor as the twenty-seventh sultan.

One man whose opinion helped shape government policy on the water community was a Dr. Hoops, the principal civil medical officer of the Straits Settlements. He visited Brunei in 1921 and wrote:

> Two-fifths of the total population of Brunei state inhabits the capital town of Brunei, well-styled the Venice of the East: for 777 of the houses within the town limits, containing 7,623 people, are raised on piles in the midstream shallows of the river. The result is not only picturesque but practical, as the question of scavenging is inexpensively and suitably solved. The river is tidal and dejects are speedily washed away.
> For water supply the river dwellers depend on the streams which run down to the river from the hills fringing the left bank between the residency and the

town. These streams have been ingeniously conducted into bamboo pipes which project over the river banks and discharge their crystal contents into jars and kerosene tins which are brought over in canoes, each morning. The Malay is by nature a riverine dweller, and is usually healthy and happy when living over the water. Apart from the space which the people would require on land, I am against moving them.

The 1921 Annual Report also contained the results of a census. Of Brunei's population of 25,000-plus, there were about 13,800 Brunei Malays, 4,700 Kedayans, 2,400 Tutongs, 1,200 Chinese, 1,100 Dusuns, 580 Bukits, 560 Muruts, 450 Belaits, 240 Dayaks (migrants from Sarawak), 200 Indians, 150 Javanese, 40 Banjarese (from Kalimantan), 35 Europeans and 20 others.

The British residents continued to encourage the Chinese to settle in Brunei for their commercial skills. Their steady influx was reflected in increasing government-controlled opium sales, said the Annual Report of 1927. That year, Brunei's capital was connected to a piped water supply, although this was not to be extended to the water community until after World War II.

Education was at first left to private interests, with a Malay teacher setting up the first school in 1913, but before long the government also became involved. Members of the royal household were first sent to an ordinary school in 1931. By 1938, there were 21 Malay vernacular, four Chinese and three private English primary schools. Secondary level education had to be obtained overseas.

III
From Rags to Riches

While 1929 is best known as the year the Great Depression began, for Brunei it represented a wonderful change of fortune. Oil was discovered at the western end of the sultanate by the Shell group's British Malayan Petroleum Company after many years of prospecting. According to company legend, the right place to drill was identified by a pair of oil executives riding bicycles down the hard-packed beach that served as the road between the tiny settlements of Kuala Belait and Seria. When they reached the mouth of the Seria River they were so exhausted they sprawled on the sand for a rest—and one of them sniffed oil and recommended a survey that led to the discovery of the Seria field.

Within a few years oil revenues were flowing into Brunei, and the debt to Malaya was paid off by 1936. It was during this period that the water community became known as Kampong Ayer, and the capital on land as Brunei Town. The growing oil industry meanwhile attracted many new Chinese as well as Indian and Sarawak Dayak immigrants, who settled in Kuala Belait or Seria to work in the oilfields or open businesses.

World War II halted the march to prosperity despite the fact that Brunei became part of the Japanese Co-prosperity Sphere. Oil production facilities were ravaged first by the retreating British in late 1941, and then even more thoroughly by the Japanese occupiers as their defeat by the Allied forces became imminent. Although the Japanese left Sultan Ahmad Tajuddin on the throne, life was harsh and fear-filled, especially for the Chinese due to historical Japanese-Chinese enmity. All white persons were rounded up and sent to prisoner-of-war camps (mainly Batu Lintang near Kuching, the Sarawak capital), although for the first year or two a European priest was allowed to stay on and two doctors—Canadian George Graham in Brunei Town and Australian M. C. Clarke in Kuala Belait—to practice.

In his memoirs published in 1984, Dr. Clarke recalled an incident which happened during a visit to Brunei Town:

Graham stood in high favor with the Sultan of Brunei. One afternoon, he and I were summoned to the Istana (palace). The Private Secretary showed us to a large polished table on the first floor verandah. In a glass-fronted cabinet was a magnificent display of Brunei silverware. On the walls were swords, krises, food covers and other decorative pieces. Further along the verandah was a throne with colored curtains draped about it.

Presently the Sultan joined us. His attire acknowledged the Malay love for brilliant colors. In his early thirties, he was slightly built, with an aquiline nose, large, humorous eyes and a scanty, rather whimsical moustache. He was not happy about the Japanese invasion. Rather than doing nothing, he became deliberately busy—he gambled, drank and made love, fulltime! He commiserated with Graham about the loss of his personal possessions, including a car which had been turned upside down in the river by the Japanese. Graham told the Sultan that his salary did not reach him, but I don't think this impressed the Sultan who never personally handled any money at all. After 15 minutes conversation we accompanied the Sultan to his private office. The Sultan removed his coat and opened a gap in his shirt between two buttoms. Graham applied his stethoscope to the small area of golden brown skin so revealed. For some seconds there was dead silence; then the Sultan burst out laughing. "There's nothing the matter with me! I only called you to have a talk. Now tell me, when is Mr. Pengilly coming back?" Mr. Pengilly had been the Resident, Brunei, when war broke out.

All-out fighting reached the sultanate only towards the end of the war, when Brunei Town was leveled by bombs rained down by Allied planes. Kampong Ayer, fortunately, was left virtually untouched because the Japanese had put all their important installations on land. Actual liberation began on June 10, 1945, when Allied troops landed at Muara.

After the war, the British gave top priority to restoring oil production. A start was made at rebuilding Brunei Town, and some of the bombed-out Chinese shopkeepers resettled in Kampong Ayer, at the water's edge in the ward of Sultan Lama, which remains the only part of Kampong Ayer with a significant concentration of Chinese.

A Wily New Sultan

Sultan Ahmad Tajuddin died in June 1950, leaving only daughters. The rather revolutionary idea of putting one of them on the throne was seriously considered, but in the end the deceased's younger brother Omar Ali Saifuddin III (there were 10 brothers and sisters in all) became the twenty-eighth in the royal line at the age of 35. He had spent four years gaining a secondary education in Malaya, returning to Brunei in 1936 to work at the junior officer level in several government departments. He was knighted by Queen Elizabeth in 1953 (after which he was commonly referred to as Sir Omar) and proved to be an Anglophile. Impressed by the venerable London taxi, he imported one for his personal use, and also built a museum (opened in 1972) displaying memorabilia of his hero, Sir Winston Churchill. But he was strong-willed and wily enough to maintain Brunei's status as an hereditary sultanate in the face of intense British pressure to both democratize and become but one part in some larger territorial entity.

The first concrete move in the latter direction had come in 1948, when the governor of Sarawak was also given the duties of Brunei high commissioner, and Sultan Ahmad Tajuddin signed an agreement accepting Sarawak (mostly British) officers to advise in the administration of Brunei. North Borneo and Sarawak had both become British colonies following the war, as their "owners" voluntarily handed them over because of the prohibitive costs of post-war reconstruction. As early as the 1930s it had been proposed that these two territories and Brunei be merged, and this idea was revived in 1953. It appealed to the British as a way to establish a political grouping large enough to stand on its own and eventually be given independence, thus allowing them to bow out gracefully having done their duty by introducing democratic government to a once "uncivilized" part of the world. The fact that Brunei was not a colony, but a protectorate retaining a strong voice on its future, was to prove a stumbling block.

Complicating matters were the winds of nationalism which blew up throughout Southeast Asia after the war (the Japanese, after all, had shown that the white men were no infallible super race). Nationalism was little more than a breeze in British Borneo with political awareness slow to grow – and then barely at all among the illiterate rural majority – but events were also pushed along by the vigorous independence movement over in Malaya as well as British strategic considerations.

In Brunei, Sultan Sir Omar realized that independence was the trend, but he also knew that his sultanate, with its oil wealth, was a tempting prize and still very much in need of British protection. The solution was to continue as a British protectorate but with internal self-rule based on a constitution (Brunei's first) for which preparations began in 1953. The British pressed for a program of democratization, which the sultan worked to make as gradual as possible. As a first step in introducing Bruneians to the rudiments of participatory government, District Advisory Councils were set up in 1954 (with members appointed by the sultan). The District Councils could send representatives to the State Council to air the people's views. The next step came two years later, when a law was passed establishing Urban and District councils to run certain local affairs – but this was not implemented because the local representatives were unwilling to take on the fiscal responsibility.

In addition to the talk of political reforms, there were more concrete steps to head off potential discontent through the channeling of oil money into social programs. Roads, schools and medical facilities sprang up and assistance to farmers was increased. In 1955, citizens over 60 years of age began receiving old-age pensions on a non-contributory basis, and the infirm were paid monthly allowances. The face of the capital was transformed with an array of impressive buildings, including a new palace, the Istana Darul Hana, for the sultan and his family. The grandest building of all, which showed that Brunei still had the ability to think big, was Southeast Asia's biggest mosque. Built next to Kampong Ayer (and named, naturally, after Sir Omar), it has a 166-foot minaret, a gold dome covered with more than three million pieces of Venetian mosaic, Italian marble floors, Shanghai granite exterior walls, and an escalator to take royal family members up to their own private prayer room. Completed in 1958, it remains a source of great pride for most of the Muslim population.

The social benefits and the steady trickling down of oil wealth gave the average Bruneian an exceptionally high standard of living by Asian standards, as reflected in the changing appearance of Kampong Ayer. Prospering water villagers put corrugated iron over their heads instead of *nipah* palm leaves, and the community became electrified and water-supplied. There were still quite a few sun-hatted *padian* peddling from their little boats, but the expansion of Kampong Ayer's network of plank (and now concrete) walkways led to most villagers doing their shopping on land. To relieve overcrowding, the government offered interest-free house loans to those wanting to shift to land, and many who did so were helped to start rubber gardens. Rubber was an important part of Brunei's economy until recently, but very few trees are tapped these days because salaried jobs are so much better paying.

Increased spending power led to rapidly growing purchases of manufactured goods and packaged foods — and an accompanying pollution problem. Water villagers customarily tossed their refuse in the water and defecated there as well, relying on the tide to carry it all out to sea. But the boxes, tin cans, plastic wrappers, food leftovers and so on discarded by a growing population have become so great in quantity that much of the garbage ends up left behind on fly-infested mud banks or floating in backwater corners of the water village where the tide deposits it rather than taking it away. Government calls to the people to take their garbage to dump sites on land have failed to change old habits, and so far there has been no move to introduce either a collection service or a sewage system (either undertaking would probably be prohibitively expensive considering Kampong Ayer's dispersed, over-the-water character).

Top: Plank walkway in Kampong Ayer (new Diplomatic Services headquarters is on hill in the background). Bottom: An elderly Brunei Malay woman making traditional glutinous rice cakes (wrapped in palm leaves) — Kampong Ayer kitchens now have modern appliances such as refrigerators.

Azahari's Political Party

Brunei's backwater atmosphere began to be roiled in 1956 with the formation of its first political party, the socialist Brunei People's Party (BPP). This was the creation of Sheik A. M. Azahari, a firebrand orator with an egomaniacal streak. He was born in Labuan of Arab-Malay parentage, and as a young man during World War II was sent by the Japanese to study veterinary science in Java. But instead he joined the anti–Japanese resistance, and after the war participated in the Indonesian revolution against the Dutch.

In the early 1950s Azahari tried his hand at various businesses in Singapore, traveling frequently to Brunei, where he tried to form a political party demanding independence — and was thrown in jail for six months by the British for organizing what was probably the sultanate's first political demonstration.

All of Azahari's businesses (which included movie production, printing, and construction, among others) seem to have failed, which raised the question of where he was getting his hundreds of thousands of dollars. Some of the money apparently came from the sultan himself, but the motivation remains a secret, although it may well have had something to do with using Azahari as leverage against the British by raising the specter of a socialist takeover.

Azahari finally got his party registered in the middle of 1956, and by early the next year his energetic organizational efforts had recruited an astonishing 16,000 members (or so the BPP claimed), about one-fifth of the population. Most were non-noble Brunei Malays, undoubtedly reflecting dissatisfaction with the ancient hereditary class system. Although the party manifesto promised to "safeguard the position of the Sultan and his heirs" it was also implied that the people would eventually be given the reins of government.

Azahari also appealed to Malay nationalism by speaking of the formation of an independent Malay nation covering the whole Malay archipelago (conveniently ignoring the fact that the Malays were very much the minority in Borneo).

The populist rhetoric of the BPP wasn't acceptable to Sir Omar, for he wanted to continue to rule supreme, paternalistically bestowing whatever reforms he deemed fit — and no more. One such reform followed the attainment of independence by the Federation of Malaya in August 1957. Jolted by the BPP's demands and its support by so many Bruneians, the sultan announced elections for unofficial members of the District Councils. However, the BPP boycotted the elections because they were to be held in the "traditional manner," and they were postponed indefinitely.

Another early clash was over the British proposal to merge Brunei,

North Borneo and Sarawak. As presented in 1958, it called for each of the territories to handle its own finances (an enticement for Brunei as it would not have to share its oil wealth), while the central government would control defense, foreign relations, communications and internal security. A colonial officer would initially head the government, but independence would eventually be granted.

Sir Omar rejected the merger, saying that Bruneians felt it would delay independence for Brunei. Not explicitly stated was their (and particularly the royal family's) immense pride in their ancient realm. They were afraid it would lose its unique identity through merger, and also feared the economic might of the many persons of Chinese descent who had settled in the two colonies.

The sultan said it was important to "preserve the country's position" and also stressed that Brunei was not a colony — implying that the colonies of North Borneo and Sarawak were inferior.

The BPP, on the other hand, strongly supported a merger, but not on the "colonial" terms of the British. Rather, independence should be granted immediately. However, there wasn't a great deal of outspoken support for this in politically quiescent North Borneo and Sarawak (aside from the Chinese-based Sarawak United People's Party, which like the BPP was socialist-oriented).

In any case, Azahari's plan could never have gone through, for on closer examinatin the people in the two colonies would have seen that he meant to make Brunei the main power as part of his grandiose dream of regaining Brunei's lost territories — with himself holding the reins of power.

The sultan countered with a merger plan of his own. He proposed linking up with Malaya, which would enhance Brunei's status since Malaya had gained independence in 1957. As a mark of good faith, the State Council approved a 100 million ringgit loan to Malaya at the end of 1958. However, there was a good deal of hesitancy, as usual, in taking the final step. The end of the merger idea apparently came when Malayan prime minister Tunku Abdul Rahman remarked that Brunei was too small to survive politically and economically, wounding Brunei pride.

Internal Self-Rule

One factor in Brunei hesitancy in joining Malaya was the gaining of internal self-rule in September 1959, when the constitution was finally promulgated. Under the treaty signed at the same time with the British, the 1906 agreement was revoked, returning supreme authority internally to the sultan. The British retained responsibility for defense, foreign affairs and internal security. The post of resident was abolished, while a high commissioner was appointed (the first was the resident of the time, Dennis White) to advise the sultan and his government and act as a channel of communication with Britain and other foreign countries. This also cut administrative ties with Sarawak, which had been a sore point in the sultanate.

The constitution established an Executive Council and a Legislative Council (LegCo) to replace the State Council. The Executive Council was presided over by the sultan, who had to consult it for major decisions but could disregard its advice by giving his reasons in writing. This council met only when called by the sultan, and could consider only matters he placed on the agenda. The LegCo consisted of eight ex-officio members (the sultan and other specified officials who were for the most part appointed by him), nine members nominated by the sultan, and sixteen elected members chosen from the District Councils — thus putting elected members in the minority by one, contrary to the sultan's earlier promise they would be in the majority.

Although the LegCo had less real power than the Executive Council, Sir Omar described its establishment as a "mile-stone" (which however was soon to be toppled) towards the introduction of parliamentary democracy.

The BPP, naturally enough, denounced the constitution and said it felt "insulted" at not having been consulted in its creation. In effect, the document transferred the resident's considerable powers (which were actually greater and wider-ranging than those of the nineteenth century sultans) to the sultan and various appointed officials beneath him. These included the *menteri besar* (chief minister), the head of the civil service below whom in rank came the state secretary, the attorney-general and the state financial officer.

Appointment of the latter two officials, plus the commissioner of police, head of the special branch, education officer, medical officer and state engineer, had to be jointly made by the British and the sultan, thus somewhat limiting Brunei's internal autonomy.

The following year the BPP had further cause for complaint when the Nationality Enactment was handed down. This recognized members of indigenous ethnic groups as subjects of the sultan but excluded most of the substantial immigrant population (primarily Chinese, Indonesians, Dayaks from Sarawak and Indians — plus, significantly, Labuan-born Azahari). However, they could apply for citizenship if they were resident in the sultanate for 20 out of the 25 preceding years and passed a Malay language test. The BPP maintained the residency requirement was far too long and pressed unsuccessfully for a reduction to 10 out of 15 years.

Proposal of a New Nation

The various merger proposals of the 1950s culminated in the most ambitious of all, that to create the new independent nation of Malaysia out of Malaya, Singapore and the three British Borneo territories. This was proposed by Malayan prime minister Tunku Abdul Rahman in May 1961 and accepted by the British as a way to be rid of their Borneo burden (as Sir Omar had rejected federation with Sarawak and North Borneo).

The general reaction in the two Borneo colonies was that they and possibly Brunei should federate and achieve independence before considering joining Malaya and Singapore with their much larger population and relatively more advanced socio-economic development. In Brunei Sir Omar was noncommittal at first, and the BPP was vociferously against the idea of Malaysia because it was completely at odds with Azahari's dream of ruling a new Brunei-centered nation. In addition, Tunku Abdul Rahman had openly expressed his dislike for the BPP and there was little hope it would even be allowed to rule Brunei within Malaysia.

The BPP's stand was so in tune with Bruneian feelings that within a single month, it claimed, its membership jumped from 19,000 to 26,000. One thing that stirred anti–Malaysia feelings was the posting of a large number of teachers and other government officers from Malaya to Brunei (which paid their salaries). Tunku Abdul Rahman thought this would demonstrate Malaya's good intentions, but instead it aroused suspicions (fanned by the BPP) that Malaya was out to "colonize" Brunei.

The BPP had meanwhile been nurturing a strong and vocal labor movement through the Brunei United Labor Front (BULF). Many of its officers were BPP members and Azahari was honorary advisor. The first District Council elections were due at the end of September 1961, and the BPP expected to gain most if not all elected seats in the LegCo, where it could voice its anti–Malaysia stand. The sultan's government, however, failed to confirm the date, so the BPP and BULF jointly held large rallies in June and August of 1961.

But Sir Omar had been slowly converted to the idea of Malaysia, mainly because the British were so obviously keen to leave. He reasoned that Brunei, with only 80,000 people yet great oil wealth, could find security in the large new nation. Of particular concern at that time was the threat of communist insurgency (the communist underground was then still very strong in Malaya). His strategy to negate BPP opposition to Malaysia included delay of the elections, encouragement of pro–Malaysian parties, and appeasement of Azahari by appointing him a nominated member of the LegCo as well as a member of a commission to hear the views of the people on Malaysia. The idea of the commission, however, backfired since anti–Malaysia feelings were overwhelmingly expressed at its public hearings.

The sultan nevertheless sent a delegation to Singapore in February 1962 to sign a memorandum of understanding on Malaysia. The goal was for the new nation to come into being on August 31 the following year.

Two months later Azahari made his first appearance in the LegCo (which then consisted entirely of appointed members) and proposed a motion to recognize the "historical sovereignty" of the sultanate over North Borneo and Sarawak. Following the motion's inevitable defeat, which he blamed on the "colonial legacy" of the British, he resigned and went into self-exile in Johor with the explanation, "There can be no democratic opposition in the state."

But Azahari was brought back to active politics by the prospect of District Council elections, which were finally confirmed for the end of August 1962. This was seen as a test between the sultan and the BPP, and it was no contest. The party took 32 of the 55 seats uncontested and, with 90 percent of the electorate of 6,000 voting, lost only one of the 23 others — and that was won by an independent who later joined the BPP. Azahari, being a non-citizen, did not contest.

The British, realizing that the BPP would introduce radical measures, advised Sir Omar to postpone the new LegCo's first sitting, and this was done from September to October to November. The BPP leaders took the tack of going international to publicize their demands and put pressure on the British and Sir Omar. For example, Azahari's deputy, Zaini Haji Ahmad, led a delegation to the Philippines and returned saying that that country would drop its claim to North Borneo (which was still being pressed by the heirs of the Sulu sultan, who ceded the territory to the North Borneo Company) if the British Borneo territories were merged and given their freedom.

A LegCo sitting was finally scheduled for December 5, 1962, and the BPP submitted in advance a motion calling on Great Britain to keep Brunei out of Malaysia and instead return North Borneo and Sarawak to the sultan's control, with the new federation to gain independence the following year. The LegCo speaker, however, wrote back his refusal to place the motion on the agenda because it involved the British and Malayan governments and had nothing to do with the Brunei government.

An Abortive Revolt

"When we received that, I knew we could not stop Malaysia by constitutional means, we had no alternative. We decided to strike...," Azahari explained in a press interview a few weeks later. He was referring to the armed revolt launched by the BPP on December 8 after the LegCo had once again failed to meet.

Azahari and Zaini were safely ensconced in Manila when the order for the revolt went out. Most of the fighting was done by the BPP's ragtag underground military arm, the North Kalimantan National Army (Kalimantan is the Indonesian name for Borneo), which had been secretly training in the jungle in Brunei as well as across the border in Indonesian Kalimantan. It was apparently hoped that a popular uprising would follow, spreading from Brunei into the two British colonies. But there was in fact little anti–British feeling there, as colonization was undertaken not for economic exploitation but more for strategic considerations in the uncertain post-war era. And Azahari didn't win any friends by declaring himself the prime minister of his dream nation of the Unitary State of North Kalimantan – a move which was certainly not based on the people's will, which he had always said must be obeyed. As a result, there was minor armed support for the revolt only in the North Borneo towns of Weston and Sipitang and the Sarawak districts of Limbang and Lawas, all areas near Brunei with strong traditional ties to the sultanate.

Although the announced purpose of the revolt was to drive out the British, Sir Omar felt it was directed against him and his rule as well, and he denounced it from the Brunei Town police station where the British had taken him and his family for safety. The Treaty of Protection was invoked, and the British flew in nearly 2,000 troops, mostly Gurkhas, from Singapore. The revolt was crushed in a matter of days, and more than 2,000 suspected rebels, almost all of them young Brunei Malay non-noble males, were rounded up. Most were released over the ensuing months after pledging loyalty to the sultan, but many others refused to take the pledge and were held for longer periods without being charged with any crime, as allowed under British-inspired emergency regulations imposed in response to the revolt. More than 30 rebels languished in prison for over 20 years before finally taking the pledge; by 1989 only a couple of detainees remained.

The traumatic effects of the revolt radically altered the situation in British Borneo. An important factor was the perception of foreign hands at work. Although the Philippines government was not involved, Azahari reportedly had the support of a Filipino company, the Kiram Corporation, which had obtained the rights to the claim for North Borneo from heirs of the sultan of Sulu. Azahari was said to have agreed to recognize the property rights (but not the sovereignty) of Kiram, and this led to an outcry in North Borneo over his arrogance in using the colony as a bargaining chip.

But the main concern over foreign involvement was directed at Indonesia under Sukarno, whose socialist rhetoric was anathema to the British and Sir Omar. There were strong suspicions that Indonesians (although perhaps without the knowledge of the top leaders) had encouraged the revolt. Sukarno himself was certainly sympathetic towards it, as shown by Indonesia's granting of asylum to Azahari and some of his followers. This, plus forthright noises from the giant to the south about gobbling up British Borneo, made the people of Sarawak and North Borneo start to see joining Malaysia as a means of survival, and also strengthened Sir Omar's resolve to join the new nation. The sultan was understandably incensed by Indonesia's stance, and he cut off relations; it took nearly two decades for these to be restored.

The revolt therefore achieved the opposite of its intended effect by strengthening pro–Malaysia feelings. And instead of making Brunei a parliamentary democracy, it gave the sultan an excellent excuse to delay political reforms on security grounds. Rather, emergency regulations giving the sultan's government wide powers, including detention without trial, have remained in force. The BPP was outlawed, and political activity was never revived except for one brief period in the mid–1960s.

Another important effect of the revolt was a big jump in public spending to boost security in two ways. On one hand, oil revenues were poured into a wide range of medical, education, welfare and infrastructure projects in order to dampen the obvious discontent of many residents. And on the other, the security forces were lavishly funded to counter both internal and external threats.

The Malaysia Two-Step

Negotiations with Malaya over Brunei's entry into Malaysia began in earnest in March 1963, and Sir Omar came away saying that all matters of substance had been resolved. Final agreement was supposed to come in June, but instead the sultan found Malaya making what were to him new and unacceptable demands. It appears the main sticking point was control of Brunei's oil wealth. The sultan had said he would voluntarily contribute 40 million ringgit a year (out of a national income of 90 million ringgit) to the federal government and found it offensive when the Malayans wanted to make it compulsory. It was also accepted that Brunei would have control of its oil revenues for 10 years; Malaya insisted on federal control after that, while Brunei wanted the matter to come up for renegotiation. And in June, Malaya demanded that the federal government have the right to impose immediate taxes on any new oil or mineral finds in Brunei, which was unacceptable to Sir Omar. There are suspicions that on this latter issue, the Royal Dutch Shell Group (which was of course against the idea of federal taxes on its Brunei operations) played petro-politics by trumpeting the discovery of large offshore oil deposits, in hopes of hardening the positions of both sides. It has even been suggested that the oil strike made the British themselves suddenly start advising the sultan to stay out of Malaysia rather than jeopardizing Royal Dutch Shell's interests, in which there was a major British stake.

Another sticking point was Sir Omar's position on the Council of Rulers. Of the 11 states of what was to become Peninsular Malaysia, nine had hereditary sultans who were automatically council members. The idea was that the sultans would take turns being Malaysia's figurehead king for five-year terms. Sir Omar was told that as the Council's newest member, he would be at the bottom in terms of precedence, which one member of the Brunei delegation described as "too damaging to be acceptable." The talks broke down despite two summit meetings between Sir Omar and Tunku Abdul Rahman. Brunei nevertheless sent a delegation to the signing ceremony for Malaysia in London that July, but hopes of a last-minute solution failed to materialize.

The real reasons for Brunei opting out remain unclear. As recently as 1983, Tunku Abdul Rahman and Sir Omar made conflicting statements to the press. The Tunku claimed it was because Sir Omar wanted to be Malaysia's first king but this couldn't be guaranteed, while Sir Omar maintained it was because of oil issues and Malaya's refusal to stick to previously negotiated terms. And there may very well have been other unspoken considerations — continuing reluctance to be but one state among many, decreased power for the royal family as Malaysia was to be a parliamentary democracy, the people's opposition as expressed in the revolt, and new oil discoveries that would ensure Brunei's economic viability.

Pressure for Reform

Although Malaysia relieved the British of North Borneo and Sarawak, they were still left with Brunei, where they began pressuring Sir Omar to introduce democratic reforms, delegate more powers to his underlings and start preparing for full independence as early as possible. Talks led to the sultan agreeing to once again hold elections for the LegCo, which would be composed of 10 elected and 11 appointed members. He also agreed to introduce a ministerial form of government with 6 ministers and 4 assistant ministers, and promised to eventually expand the number of elected LegCo members to 20 and have a fully-elected Cabinet. In the meantime, a Council of Ministers replaced the old Executive Council.

Brunei's final experiment with democracy came in March 1965, when general elections for the LegCo were held. Many of the 36 who stood were independents because of the weakness of the few political parties; of the 10 elected, 3 were former Azahari supporters.

But real changes to the system were not made. The British renewed pressure on Sir Omar when he went to London after the elections, but he responded: "I have said all along that constitutional changes must be brought about step by step. That is a sure way of avoiding trouble." His only concession was to appoint two of the four assistant ministers from among those elected to the LegCo.

Local politicians once again became a source of pressure when the parties merged in August 1966 to form the Brunei People's Independence Party led by former BPP vice-president H. A. Hapidz Laksamana. This new party soon sent a memorandum to the British accusing them of delaying Brunei's independence — but the reply, perhaps to their surprise, was that Great Britain was keen for Brunei to achieve independence as soon as possible. This put the burden on Sir Omar. In March 1967 the party asked the sultan to state his stand, but he declined to reply. The party then sent a delegation to see him, but he wouldn't meet them — but the British High Commissioner received them, further making Sir Omar look the odd man out. He angrily flew to London, but the British stayed firm in saying they wanted to see changes in Brunei, after which they would leave.

On October 4, 1967, Sir Omar made a wholly unexpected move — he announced his abdication as sultan of Brunei and named as successor his eldest son (full name: Muda Hassanal Bolkiah Mu'izzaddin Waddaulah). No reason was given, although in an interview four years later, Sir Omar claimed that he'd made the decision a decade ahead of time. "I prayed to God (in 1957) that when I reached 50 and my son had completed his studies I should hand over," he said. "This was not a secret. I had expressed it several times." In fact, Sir Omar turned 50 in 1964, but explained in the interview that his son had yet to finish school at that time. Yet there was undoubtedly an element of suddenness in the abdication, for Muda Hassanal Bolkiah, then 21, had to be whisked back from England, where he was a cadet at the Royal Military Academy at Sandhurst, to take the throne.

The real reason for the abdication had to do with friction with the British. According to a report issued a few months later by the Economist Intelligence Unit, headquartered in London, two theories were current:

> One was that he was resigning in protest against the transfer from Brunei of the British High Commissioner, Mr. F. D. Webber. (Sir Omar is said to have told the British Government that he would not have anyone other than Mr. Webber as envoy to his State.)
>
> The other was that British pressure for constitutional reform was becoming too much for the Sultan. He has been refusing for the past three years to consent to the introduction of ministerial government into the Sultanate, although a succession of Commonwealth Secretaries have pressed him to consider it. It is thought that Prince Hassanal may prove more responsive to advice from Britain, but as a protectorate Brunei remains fully responsible for its internal affairs.

At this time, the Council of Ministers was the most important of the various councils as it handled all policy matters. It met in private and was presided over by the sultan, who appointed all its 11 members except for the British high commissioner. Hence the sultan's word was virtually law.

But hopes that the new sultan had absorbed British governmental ideals proved illusory. He showed relatively little interest in actually governing the sultanate for at least the first dozen years of his rule, while his father's hand could be discerned in almost every major decision. Hence events supported the theory that Sir Omar abdicated to deflect British pressure for democratization. He could then claim that his son, the new sultan, needed a few years to learn the ropes and solidify his rule before any changes could be introduced—all the while acting himself as the power behind the throne. He took the title Seri Begawan Sultan, and the name of the capital was subsequently changed from Brunei Town to Bandar Seri Begawan (*bandar* means town).

A minor change in relations with Great Britain came in 1971, when a new treaty was signed giving Brunei responsibility for its own internal security. The British, however, continued to provide a defense umbrella and handle external relations.

Malaysian Pressure, Too

Relations with Malaysia had meanwhile deteriorated, apparently due to pique in Kuala Lumpur over Brunei's refusal to join the new nation. In early 1964, Tunku Abdul Rahman recalled the hundreds of officers posted in the sultanate; Brunei responded by recruiting replacements in the Philippines and Great Britain. At about the same time, Malaysia decided to terminate the board which had been issuing a common currency for Malaya, Singapore and British Borneo and pass its functions to the country's national bank (Bank Negara)—without offering Brunei any voice in making policy. The sultanate therefore began issuing its own currency (printed and minted in England).

On the other hand, Brunei developed very close ties with the region's other "odd man out," Singapore, after the latter was expelled from Malaysia in August 1965. The Malaysian national airline was also broken up, into Singapore International Airlines (SIA) and Malaysian Airlines System (MAS), but Brunei gave landing rights only to SIA. Brunei and Singapore also worked out an agreement putting their currencies at par.

Then came the strange affair of Zaini Haji Ahmad, the BPP's deputy leader. After the failure of the Brunei rebellion, he renounced Azahari and sought asylum in Hong Kong, but the British turned him over to Brunei and he was jailed at Jerudong. Azahari had meanwhile taken refuge in Malaysia, although he was to later shift to Indonesia. In 1966, Zaini announced he was willing to renounce his Brunei citizenship if he was exiled, and Malaysia let it be known it would accept him. Seven years later Zaini and seven other political detainees escaped to Sarawak — accompanied by the jail's chief warder, who happened to be a Malaysian, thus raising suspicions it was all engineered by Malaysia's Special Branch.

The BPP had been allowed to open an office in Kuala Lumpur, from which it agitated for Brunei's democratization and full independence. These calls were supported by Malaysia, which in 1975 sponsored a BPP delegation to present its case to the United Nations Committee on Decolonization. Towards the end of that year, the United Nations General Assembly passed a resolution endorsed by Australia, Indonesia, the Philippines and Thailand, which called on Great Britain:

> as the administering Power, to take all steps within its competence to facilitate expeditiously the holding of free democratic elections by the appropriate government authorities in Brunei in consultation with and under the supervision of the United Nations in accordance with the inalienable rights of the people of Brunei to self-determination and independence, and further calls, prior to the elections, for the lifting of the ban on all political parties and the return of all political exiles to Brunei so that they can participate freely and fully in the election.

Brunei's response was orchestrated by Sir Omar. The Limbang claim was revived, and there was an air of crisis when some people in the district signed petitions that they preferred to be part of Brunei (echoing the tactic of Sir Charles Brooke shortly before he seized Limbang for Sarawak). The chief minister of Sarawak led anti-Brunei demonstrations, and Brunei banned the entry of Sarawak government vehicles. And a large number of Brunei students studying in Peninsular Malaysia were recalled.

The outside pressure appears to have made the sultanate's rulers dig in their heels all the harder. They once again made the LegCo an entirely appointed body, and with their territory surrounded and partitioned by Sarawak — a state of a hostile nation — they valued British protectorate status all the more. It was only after Malaysia reversed its pro-BPP policy that the British could induce Sir Omar and Sir Hassanal (who was knighted by Queen Elizabeth during a visit to Brunei in 1972) to accept full independence — but only on their own terms, leaving them in full power.

The thaw in relations with Malaysia followed Tun Hussein Onn's succession as that country's third prime minister in 1975 (the second had been Tun Abdul Razak). He disagreed with the confrontational policy of his predecessors and sent out peace feelers in early 1977, and two years later broke the ice by attending a royal wedding in Brunei. The following year, Sir Hassanal went to Kuala Lumpur to attend the installation of the new Malaysian king, a polo-playing friend.

An Independence Agreement

The British had long been pushing Brunei towards independence (in part to put a stop to charges of colonialism), and on January 7, 1979, a Treaty of Friendship and Cooperation was finally signed under which this significant event was to be achieved by the end of 1983 (the actual date was later fixed for January 1, 1984).

Another significant event in 1979 was the death of Sir Omar's wife. A long mourning period was declared during which sporting events were not allowed and state television stopped broadcasting entertainment shows. Sir Omar subsequently seemed to lose some of his old interest in the running of the sultanate and Sir Hassanal became more active, making inspection tours of government departments and holding meet-the-people sessions in Kampong Ayer.

During the run-up to independence, and especially from 1981 on, preparations were made at a rapid pace on both the foreign and local fronts. For example, there were moves to strengthen the government bureaucracy. A sound technocrat, Pehin Dato Haji Abdul Aziz, was appointed acting chief minister in October 1981, and early the next year an anti-corruption bureau was established directly under the sultan to root out the corruption that had become endemic in the bureaucracy. This was initially headed by P. Rajaratnam, a retired Singapore deputy commissioner of police whose drowning death at a beach near Bandar Seri Begawan was the most sensational event of 1984. The coroner who conducted the inquest into the apparent suicide returned an open verdict because, although there was no sign of foul play, it was revealed that Rajaratnam seemed to have become severely depressed after allegedly being threatened by high Education Department officials who were under investigation. Indeed, attempts to investigate and prosecute any but minor officials were said to have been consistently blocked by men in the upper echelons of the government.

On the legal front, old laws were updated and new ones were introduced, often along the lines of those in force in Malaysia and Singapore, where the legal systems are also British-derived. Following the lead of the new international Law of the Sea, the sultanate's territorial waters were extended from 3 to 12 miles and the fisheries limit to 200 miles. Brunei also got a Merchant Shipping Enactment similar to those of most Commonwealth countries plus a Post Office Bill allowing the opening of suspected seditious items.

A welter of road and building projects were rushed to completion, notably the 35,000-seat Hassanal Bolkiah National Stadium equipped with a huge state-of-the-art electronic scoreboard, and the sultan's mammoth new palace, both of which were to be main venues for independence celebrations. Although independence came on January 1, 1984, the celebrations didn't begin until February 23, to allow for the finishing touches to be put on the palace. As late as the previous December, a Brunei team had hit Chicago's Merchandise Mart with a budget of $1.6 million to buy palace furnishings to be rushed to Brunei by chartered jet.

A flurry of initiatives also took place in the field of foreign relations, the most significant of these being the strengthening of ties with the five members of the Association of Southeast Asian Nations (ASEAN, comprising Indonesia, Malaysia, the Philippines, Singapore and Thailand). Significantly, the British, although still officially responsible for foreign relations, let the Brunei government play the leading role, and contrary to previous practice, all-Brunei delegations became the norm for overseas missions.

The ice on Indonesia relations was broken thanks mainly to President Suharto, who in contrast to his predecessor Sukarno does not go for expansionist diplomacy but stresses internal stability and economic development. President Suharto is credited with proposing in 1980 that Brunei become ASEAN's sixth member to Singapore prime minister Lee Kuan Yew, a longtime friend of Sir Omar and Sir Hassanal. The following year, the sultan visited Singapore where the proposal was discussed, and later went to Indonesia itself where he was given a warm welcome.

Also that year he made his first official visit to Malaysia (he had, however, previously made a number of unofficial visits to attend royal weddings or play polo). But instead of going to the capital, Kuala Lumpur, he went to Sabah, apparently in part to show his continuing displeasure with Sarawak and in particular its ceremonial head of state, Tan Sri Haji Abdul Rahman Yaakub (who had organized anti-Brunei rallies in the mid-1970s while chief minister). However, Haji Abdul Rahman later visited Brunei several times and had cordial audiences with both Sir Omar and Sir Hassanal. Malaysia's deputy prime minister Datuk Musa Hitam came calling in 1982 and prime minister Datuk Sri Dr Mahathir Mohamad the following year with offers of places for Bruneians in various training institutions.

Top-level visits were also exchanged with Thailand and the Philippines, both of which have significant economic ties with the sultanate. Thailand traditionally provides about 90 percent of its rice, while Filipino companies have won a large number of construction contracts (including the palace) on which a great many Filipinos work. Members of the Brunei royal family also have close business and polo-playing ties with Filipino corporate dynasties.

By the time of independence, Brunei had exchanged diplomats with all its future ASEAN brethren. Here at last was a larger grouping which Sir Omar and Sir Hassanal were only too happy to join. Its international standing had grown greatly since its inception in 1967, particularly through its united and effective diplomatic stand against Vietnam's invasion of and stationing of troops in Kampuchea; the United Nations has consistently supported ASEAN's motions on Kampuchea and refused to recognize the Vietnamese-installed regime. ASEAN's anti-communism and commitment to non-interference in the internal affairs of member nations are comforting to tiny Brunei, nestled as it is at the boundary of giant Indonesia and "big brother" Malaysia which only a few years ago keenly supported drastic changes within the sultanate. Now they have formally recognized the status quo and there is also the prospect of military cooperation.

As independence approached, Brunei was also wooed by the United States, Australia, Japan and South Korea, all of which were given permission to set up diplomatic missions. All have major economic stakes in Brunei through trade, construction work or participation in the all-important oil industry.

Apron-String Traumas

But cutting the apron strings with Mother Britain proved to be a bit traumatic. The main cause of tension was disagreement over the status of a battalion of some 1,000 British army Gurkhas, paid for by Brunei, based at Seria to guard key oil installations.

Brunei leaders seem to have an almost mystical belief in the fighting prowess of the Gurkhas who so efficiently snuffed out the 1962 rebellion, and were very keen to keep them in the sultanate after independence. The British were quite willing to allow this, despite the possibility of being charged with maintaining a "neo-colonial" military presence, because in exchange Brunei could provide continued use of superb jungle training facilities. The problem was that the sultan wanted a degree of control over the Gurkha battalion, although exactly what sort of control was never revealed. According to some press reports, he wanted command of the battalion — a demand which two British government ministers failed to get him to drop during visits in March and April 1983. The British were unyielding; the sultan might be footing the bill for the Gurkhas, but there was no way they would give him the power to use British units to suppress internal dissent (not that he would, but giving him the power to do so would cause an uproar in Britain).

Both Brunei and Britain denied there was any rift, but events proved otherwise. That April, High Commissioner Arthur Watson was suddenly relieved of his duties and made an unannounced departure from Brunei. The British Broadcasting Corporation's world radio service speculated it was because Watson had clashed with the sultan — and within two weeks,

Radio Television Brunei stopped relaying BBC radio news broadcasts without explanation.

But a far stronger move was to come in July, when Brunei abruptly transferred control of the major portion of its foreign exchange holdings away from Britain's crown agents, who for more than a century have provided various economic services to many of the smaller territories that were once part of the British Empire. By 1983, Brunei's portfolio represented 90 percent of the investment funds managed by the agents. Although Brunei began diversifying management of its funds in 1978, the abruptness and size of the July 1983 move gave it strong political overtones. Another factor was that a few months earlier, Britisher John Lee (who had been bestowed the title of Pehin Datuk for his many years of service) retired as Brunei State financial officer, and he had been a strong supporter of the crown agents.

Differences were resolved by September, however, with Sir Hassanal dropping his demand for control of the Gurkhas, and British minister of state in the Foreign and Commonwealth Office Richard Luce visited the sultanate to sign a new defense agreement. Details were not revealed aside from acknowledging the Gurkhas would stay, under British command, and Great Britain would continue to make use of jungle-training facilities. Knowledgeable sources said the future of the Gurkhas was to be reviewed every five years (and in 1988 Brunei and Britain did indeed agree to extend the accord).

Back in the mother country there was a lot of clucking over the way Brunei was heading for independence as an anachronistic autocracy. A frequently expressed feeling in the press and on radio and television was that it was something of a national disgrace to be "granting" independence to a territory which refused to accept democracy — as otherwise what was the point of taking the sultanate under wing in the first place? Such sentiments, however, did not take account of the fact that Brunei had never been a colony, and the British simply did not have the power to impose democracy.

Time to Celebrate

Finally, the long gestation of Brunei's independence came to an end at the stroke of midnight on December 31, 1983, before the eyes of the world (through the lenses of hundreds of TV and still cameras). The auspicious evening began with special prayers in the mosques, with members of the royal family attending the packed Omar Ali Saifuddin Mosque in the capital. At about 10:30 P.M. people began gathering just across from the mosque at the new Haji Sir Omar Ali Saifuddin Park, where grandstands had been built around a large open area especially for the occasion. The crowd totaled about 30,000 an hour later when the royal family arrived in limousines following the customary escort of white police motorcycles. The grand chamberlain followed, bearing the Declaration of Independence, accompanied by 32 Royal Brunei Armed Forces regalia bearers dressed in traditional black and gold costumes with brass shields, who formed a line in front of the gilded royal dais.

The ceremony began with the state mufti, Pehin Dato Haji Ismail bin Omar Abdul Aziz, reading from the Koran, after which his Highness the Sultan and Yang Dipertuan Sir Muda Hassanal Bolkiah, clad in a military uniform, read the Declaration of Independence. Using some apparently contradictory terms, he declared Negara Brunei Darussalam (Brunei, the Abode of Peace) to be a "sovereign, democratic and independent Malay Muslim monarchy" which would be administered according to Islamic teachings. The proclamation also traced the "special treaty relationship" between Brunei and Britain which began in 1847, and said that the sultanate would pursue friendly relations with all other countries based on "the principle of mutual respect for the independence, sovereignty, equality and territorial integrity of all nations free from external interference."

Then 70-year-old Sir Omar, also in military uniform, rose from his seat to lead the crowd in thrice chanting "Allahhu Akbar" ("God is Great" — the Muslim call to prayer which echoes throughout the world five times a day). As the last cry died away, a deafening 21-cannon salute filled the air and more than a million lightbulbs strung across public buildings were switched on to the frenetic beat of *hadrah* (Malay hand drums) while fireworks burst in the black sky.

The sultan also announced a new ministerial form of government, but any hopes for even minor power-sharing went unfulfilled. All the top posts went to himself, his father and two brothers (a third brother who had been widely tipped as finance minister was left off the list due to his poor health). The sultan had earlier, however, ordered the release of three of the 30-plus political prisoners held without trial at Jerudong Prison under emergency laws imposed at the time of the 1962 rebellion. This may have been meant as a symbolic gesture auguring a liberalization of the old order, but changes have tended to remain symbolic rather than substantive.

The real celebrations began on February 23 and lasted for four days, and were conducted on such a lavish scale that the *Times* of London called them in a headline, "the Brunei party to end all parties." Kings, queens, sheiks, prime ministers and top diplomats from more than 40 countries were there. On their arrival at the airport outside the capital, they were whisked by helicopter to the Haji Omar Saifuddin Park in the center of town, where they were given military band welcomes that lasted virtually from dawn to dusk. The most distinguished among them were housed in 18 luxury villas rushed to completion just for the occasion.

King Malietua TanuMafili the Second, ruler for life of Western Samoa, provided a dash of incongruity when he arrived garbed in a jacket and tie plus a brown cloth skirt and open sandals (he also brought along a chair custom-made for his 350-pound frame). Ferdinand Marcos, then Philippine president, had the biggest entourage (120 strong including a large number of bodyguards). Representing Great Britain was Prince Charles, who brought along three truckloads of luggage and his polo manager (for a friendly knockabout at the sport of royalty with the sultan). Instead of flying in, Saudi Arabian tycoon Adnan Khashoggi cruised up the Brunei River in his 300-foot yacht, the *Nabila*, which was widely felt to be the world's most luxurious (its amenities include a discotheque and a helicopter pad), augmenting its owner's billionaire aura. Sir Hassanal was so impressed with the vessel that he bought it (he would later sell it to American real estate magnate Donald Trump for $30 million).

A main highlight of Brunei's first National Day celebrations was a mass rally of nearly two hours at the Hassanal Bolkiah National Stadium, with Sir Hassanal in the middle of the royal dais flanked by the King of Malaysia on his right and Prince Charles on his left. Thousands of Brunei residents had begun practicing their roles months in advance, and it was all organized by members of committees and subcommittees whose names took 18 typewritten pages to list. The human formations that went through their paces (to commentaries in both Malay and English) presented idealized images of the way of life and aspirations of the people of Brunei. The members of the young farmer's contingent wore yellow to represent strength of character, green for fertility and yellow and black for perseverance. A large group of young women created a rotating floral pattern as they danced, and young fishermen rowed in unison as they crouched down outlining the shape of a Bruneian boat. A group also took to the field to form the state crest, said to represent the unity of the people in upholding the new nation's aspirations and sovereignty.

The festivities also included a mass display of *silat* (the Malay art of self-defense) and march-pasts by contingents from the public and private sectors, and there was the throbbing of hundreds of *hadrah* and a flip-card display spelling out *Allahhu akbar*. Then the 30,000-plus Bruneians in attendance took a pledge before the sultan to be united as a nation guided by Islam and the monarchy. The rally ended with the release of 1,984 balloons (representing the year on the Western calendar) and 1,404 pigeons (representing the year on the Muslim calendar).

Another major event came as the mahogany doors of the mammoth new palace, the Istana Nurul Iman, were opened to the public for the first time. More than 4,300 guests passed through those doors one night to dine on chicken stuffed with African mango, prawns cooked in a hot chili sauce and a host of other exotic dishes ladled out by white-gloved waiters.

IV
Brunei's People

Brunei, unlike many multi-ethnic nations, does not suffer from open racial and religious strife. Economic prosperity for virtually all is undoubtedly a major reason for this happy situation, although the people themselves give the impression of being generally tolerant and slow to turn to violence.

The population is about 230,000; the male-female ratio is 3:2 because more than a quarter of the people are short-term immigrant workers who are almost all men, although many do bring their wives and children. According to government figures, the ethnic breakdown is 55 percent Brunei Malay, 12 percent other indigenes, 26 percent Chinese (although some Chinese leaders claim the real figure is at least 30 percent), and 7 percent others. Some 54 percent live in the Brunei-Muara District, 33 percent in Belait, 10 percent in Tutong and 3 percent in Temburong.

The Brunei Malays are distinguished by having what is probably Borneo's most highly stratified society. It is likely that this stratification and Brunei's traditional form of government as a hereditary sultanate developed hand-in-hand: hereditary nobles held the highest posts, and their highly centralized rule proved able to build empires and draw in wealth, which in turn strengthened the system. In the Brunei mind, prosperity has always flowed from the sultan and to a lesser extent from his close relatives, and — who knows? — perhaps it will always be so. Certainly in Brunei today the sultan is the undoubted supreme authority, enjoying the sort of respect and loyalty that almost unlimited wealth and power command. So this chapter describing the people of Brunei will begin at the top.

The Royal Family

Sir Hassanal is reckoned to be the twenty-ninth sultan in a royal line that, in the opinion of some scholars, stretches further back in time than

those of any of the world's 28 other remaining monarchs. The present
sultan may well have more power at his disposal than his predecessors, in
ironic contrast to the situation the British hoped to nurture through the
residency system introduced in 1906. The British residents took over many
of the powers and responsibilities not only of the sultan, but also of the
various traditional offices held by his relatives. The constitution of 1959
which brought internal independence effectively transferred these powers
and responsibilities to the sultan alone. The system of traditional offices
held by what has been termed the "core nobility" has been retained, but the
long titles are ceremonial. Virtually all the real power is held by the sultan
and a handful of close relatives, who have yet to give any indication of
allowing political parties to vie for power.

Some observers feel, however, that some form of democracy,
probably with the sultan remaining the ultimate authority, is more likely
to be introduced now that Sir Omar has passed from the scene. His death
on September 7, 1986, shortly before his seventy-second birthday, brought
to an end a sad struggle for power with his number one son which
developed as the latter gradually matured and sought to take the reins he
had ostensibly been handed in 1967. Sir Hassanal initially accepted that his
father would be the power behind the throne but by the early 1980s was
asserting his authority in ways that clearly upset the old man; by the last
year or two of his life they were not even on speaking terms. One source
of friction was that Sir Omar was a pious Muslim and disapproved of the
playboy images and profligate spending of some of his sons. There were
clashes over government policy as well, all exacerbated by the father's failing health and accompanying signs of senility.

The average Bruneian would probably never have had an inkling of
the split within the royal family had it not been for several puzzling
statements that Sir Omar had broadcast over radio and television. One of
the statements said nothing more than that Sir Hassanal had *not* been born
in the Istana Darul Hana as he claimed, but rather in an insignificant outlying building. Sir Hassanal subsequently ordered that none of his father's
statements could be broadcast without his approval. This threw radio and
television personnel into an impossible situation since Sir Omar, who was
still regarded as equal if not superior in power, responded by personally
delivering what he wanted read over the air and staying in the studio to
ensure it was broadcast.

Death came after a long illness; the cause was not announced, but Sir
Omar was said to have suffered from diabetes for a number of years. His
body lay in state for a day at the Istana Nurul Iman, where it was placed
in a three-tiered catafalque surrounded by royal yellow pillows on which
his numerous medals and decorations, bestowed mainly by fellow royalty,
were displayed. In line with tradition, the cortege bearing the coffin to the

The late Omar Ali Saifuddin, father of the sultan of Brunei, Hassanal Bolkiah, in ceremonial dress.

royal mausoleum, one-and-a-half miles away, was all male and proceeded on foot. The coffin was placed in a hand-drawn carriage followed by 17 soldiers bearing the treasured medals and decorations; the route was lined by thousands of Bruneians. A 40-day mourning period was observed, but after that things went a bit more smoothly in the government than they had previously when two power centers vied for control.

A Royal Cabinet

At full independence, Sir Hassanal had named himself prime minister, minister of finance and minister of internal affairs (which includes security), and his father minister of defense with responsibility for the Royal Brunei Armed Forces and the sultanate's privately recruited Gurkha Reserve Unit (not to be confused with the British Gurkha battalion stationed in Brunei). The second eldest brother, Prince Mohamed, was made foreign minister, and the youngest brother, Prince Jefri, minister of culture, youth and sports as well as deputy minister of finance. To the surprise of many people, the third eldest brother, Prince Sufri, was not named to the cabinet; this was because he suffers from throat cancer, which is never publicized.

Three other Brunei Malays (who had been the highest-ranking officials in the government before independence) were also given portfolios. Pengiran Bahrin bin Pengiran Haji Abas, the attorney-general, was appointed both minister of law and minister of communications; the former acting chief minister, Pehin Dato Haji Abdul Aziz, became minister of education and health; and the former acting state secretary, Pehin Dato Abdul Rahman Taib, was named minister of development. According to Pengiran Bahrin, the new ministerial form of government represented a streamlining of the old system. Department heads could now go straight to their respective ministers for decisions and when submitting reports, rather than doing the old two-step of going to the chief minister through the state secretary. The system has in fact improved the bureaucratic handling of many minor and routine matters, but those of greater significance are still likely to be ensnared in delays if final approval is needed from the sultan or one of the princes, who of course have many other things demanding their attention.

Independence also brought changes in royal titles. The sultan was previously referred to as His Highness the Sultan and Yang Dipertuan (the Yang Dipertuan signifying he had gone through the ritual coronation), but now His Highness was to be replaced by His Majesty. His Highness had commonly been referred to as HH for short, but this became HM. The sultan still expects to be approached with the reverential subservience displayed for his predecessors. Court officials never turn their backs on him but walk backwards out of the room, and they use the archaic court language of the Malays (which differs from normal spoken Malay mainly in the use of special terms of address between the ruler and his subjects).

Sir Hassanal's first wife is known as Her Majesty Paduka Seri Baginda Sultan and his second wife as Her Royal Highness Pengiran Isteri. The three other brothers retain their traditional vizier titles — Prince Mohamed as the Perdana Wazir, Prince Sufri as the Pengiran Pemancha and Prince Jefri as the Pengiran Digadong. And what had been the State of Brunei gained a long name for such a small country — Negara Brunei Darussalam. *Negara*

The sultan of Brunei, Hassanal Bolkiah, exchanging a greeting from his throne with a man on whom he has just bestowed a title.

in Malay means "country," indicating that the sultanate is fully independent, while *Darussalam* ("Abode of Peace") is the Arabic rendering of the title bestowed on it by an early Ming Dynasty emperor.

Born to Rule

Sir Omar grew up at a time when even such high nobles as he might start their careers at rather low levels in the civil service (first as a cadet

The sultan of Brunei, Hassanal Bolkiah, on his throne.

forest officer, then as a cadet judicial officer and finally as an administrator in the Resident's Office). His sons, however, have known only immense wealth and privilege.

Sir Hassanal's ascendance to the throne came by virtue of his having been first-born. He was educated by tutors at the Istana and also went to schools in Brunei and Kuala Lumpur. At the age of 15, in 1961, he was installed as the crown prince and invested with the family order of Darjah Kerabat First Class. Four years later he married a cousin, Pengiran Anak Saleha, the eldest daughter of the Pengiran Pemancha at that time, Haji

Muhammad Alam. The main event was attended by more than 3,000 guests and the traditional and elaborate ceremonies lasted for over a week, with the crown prince and his bride usually attired in *kain songket* (hand-woven cloth brocaded with gold or silver thread).

The crown prince was a cadet at Britain's Royal Military Academy at Sandhurst (and chafing under the strict discipline) when he was suddenly recalled to succeed his abdicating father. Accounts of events published in Brunei are careful to note that although he had yet to graduate, he had completed his training; the academy later awarded him an honorary commission. He was installed as the new ruler on October 5, 1967. According to Brunei Malay tradition, a new sultan would have to be on the throne at least a year before undergoing the ritual coronation. In Sir Hassanal's case, however, the advisory council dealing with customs ruled that the date could be advanced, and he was coronated on August 1, 1968.

The first rite was the traditional Muslim bathing ceremony at the Istana Darul Hana to the accompaniment of a 21-gun salute. The sultan then rode in an open coach drawn by 50 ceremonially attired men of the Royal Brunei Malay Regiment down streets thronged with people to the Lapau, the new ceremonial hall with a gilded interior. There, seated in chairs according to ancient codes of rank, were a host of noble officials plus such distinguished guests as the prime ministers of Malaysia and Singapore; representing Britain was the secretary of state for Wales.

His Highness was crowned by his father, who gave him the symbol of supreme power in Brunei, the *Kris Sinaga* (a wavy-edged dagger of traditional Malay style), which the sultan sheathed in the waistband of his gold tunic. The coronation was proclaimed to the waiting crowds outside by the firing of a small cannon. The sultan and now Yang Dipertuan was then borne in procession through the streets of Brunei Town as cannon booms and fireworks filled the air. The lavishness of the ceremonies and the number of traditional officials installed (both apparently on a larger scale than ever before) suggested that traditions would be maintained in the face of technological progress financed by petroleum riches — in fact, this wealth would be used to amplify echoes of past glories. And so the cost of the sultan's mammoth new palace, completed in early 1984, was publicly justified on the basis that it would aptly symbolize Brunei's return to glory (even though it would be inhabited by only a minute fraction of the populace).

The symbols of modern Brunei royalty include fancy cars and polo sticks; a more traditional interest is that of military affairs. Like the sultan, Prince Mohamed attended Sandhurst. Sir Omar founded and nurtured Brunei's armed forces, and Sir Hassanal (the present commander in chief) often appears in public in military garb. The sultan and the princes occasionally run the latest military hardware acquisitions (such as British-made

The sultan of Brunei, Hassanal Bolkiah, in military garb (right center), next to Prince Mohamed in civilian dress.

Scorpion tanks) through their paces and are adept marksmen with a variety of small arms. Sir Hassanal is also a qualified helicopter pilot and flits around his fiefdom in one of his gold-fitted, stereo-equipped helicopters. The royal family also has at its disposal a Gulfstream jet and three big Boeings, one of which the sultan ordered fitted out in West Germany for millions against the wishes of his father who felt the project might generate bad publicity within the sultanate (it was all kept secret but rumors nevertheless got circulating). On the ground there are more than 110 gleaming sports cars and limousines to choose from, including a Bentley with a 22-carat gold-plated grille and a stretched, custom-built six-door Rolls-Royce.

The Game of Royalty

Sandhurst not only gave Sir Hassanal a military background but also introduced him to horses. Not long after becoming sultan he got his first horse which, the story goes, was allowed free entry to the Istana Darul Hana's dining room. It was only natural he would fall in love with polo, a true test of horsemanship, when introduced to the game in 1976 by his military aide-de-campe, a newly arrived British officer. For the next few years the sultan seemed to concentrate more on developing polo facilities and perfecting his skills than on ruling Brunei. In any case, Sir Omar remained committed to taking care of the more sober side of governance.

Polo fields were built at Berakas and Jerudong, with seaside Jerudong Park being developed into one of the world's best-equipped polo clubs. There are several hundred Argentinian polo ponies tended by Argentinian grooms plus some local grooms who, for the most part, had never seen a horse until their recruitment. The facilities include air-conditioned stables for sick ponies and an ultra-plush clubhouse topped by a gold-colored, star-shaped roof.

To play polo well requires a tremendous amount of dedicated practice as rider and horse must be thoroughly acquainted with each other to execute the sudden turns and stops needed to stay with the action. Sir Hassanal, Prince Mohamed and Prince Jefri (rated the best of the three) all put in the time to become good at the game, although wins by their teams often come more through the play of highly ranked Argentinian members.

A high point of the year for Brunei's polo enthusiasts (who include a fair number of military brass) used to be the annual international tournament at Jerudong. Teams would come from Singapore, Malaysia (led by some of the nine sultans of that country), the Philippines, England and even the United States. The hosts would provide the utmost in hospitality and to some extent pageantry, with an opening parade of the hundreds of ponies, each finely turned out, to the marching music of a military brass band. The sultan and his brothers frequently led teams to overseas tournaments, and at such times the airlift of equipment and dozens of ponies would take precedence over other aviation activities at Brunei's international airport.

But polo fever apparently burned itself out for the sultan. Late in 1984 the Istana issued a terse statement that there would be no international tournament at Jerudong as originally scheduled for the following February. Some observers traced the reason to an incident earlier in 1984 when the sultan sulked for days over a disputed lost game during a tournament hosted by a Malaysian sultan.

An Istana for the Record Books

The new Istana Nurul Iman symbolizes more than anything Brunei's return to a long-lost tradition of thinking big—so big that it has been deemed the world's largest residential palace currently in occupation. Sitting atop a man-made hill on a 300-acre site in clear view of Kampong Ayer,

View over a corner of Kampong Ayer towards the Brunei sultan's new palace (then under construction), the Istana Nurul Iman — the world's largest residential palace.

it is one-third of a mile long and has about two million square feet of floor space. There are so many rooms that the sultan may well never step inside them all — a total of 1,788 (plus more than 1,000 closets), which is 388 more than the previous world record holder, the Vatican Palace in Rome, according to the *Guinness Book of World Records*. The palace's throne room, as spacious as a circus tent, is also said to be lighted by the 12 biggest chandeliers in the world, each crystal colossus weighing nearly 4,500 pounds. Other special features are the inevitable gold fittings in the royal bathrooms, more than 2,000 telephones, close to two miles of air-conditioned underground passages, an air-conditioned car park with 300 spaces, and a polo practice field with air-conditioned stables.

Brunei's independence celebrations were delayed nearly two months so the new Istana could be completed and serve as a main venue for festivities. The project fell behind schedule due to complex problems of getting equipment and materials, virtually all of which were imported, on site at the right time within an extremely tight schedule. The rush to complete the palace meant that other projects, including a new hospital in the capital, had to be neglected. The Bechtel Corporation of the United States headed a team of 20 consultant companies, while Enrique Zobel's Ayala International of the Philippines led 30 contractors. Ayala imported 5,000 workers from the Philippines, housing most of them in a small city of air-conditioned trailer units they were discouraged from leaving in order to prevent untoward incidents in town (such as impregnating local lasses). When 22-carat gold leaf was being laid on the Istana's two large domes, rifle-toting guards stood watch to make sure none of the workers were tempted to make their fortune by slipping some in their pockets. Skilled workers were also brought from Yugoslavia to do the intricate mosaic work and from Italy to supervise the laying of the marble floors.

Candidate for World's Richest Man

The cost of the Istana is commonly quoted as $350 million, but some observers reckon the final total was at least $600 million. The extra millions, however, would make little difference to a man often considered to be the world's richest. Deciding on who deserves the title turns out to be a matter of definition. Although the annual *Guinness Book of World Records* does not bestow the title on Sir Hassanal, it has pointed out that he is the "least fettered" of the world's 29 remaining monarchs, and that the sultanate's billions of dollars in foreign reserves and annual oil revenues are "effectively at his personal disposal." When the first edition of the *Guinness* book to make this statement came out, in 1983, the sultan's government issued a strong protest, maintaining that the foreign reserves are controlled by the Brunei Investment Agency, with management help from various foreign financial institutions, "according to law for the benefit of the people of Negara Brunei Darussalam." The queston that then arises is who controls the Brunei Investment Agency? And who makes the laws in the absence of even an appointed Legislative Council? Who, in the end, decides how the money is spent?

The issue of determining the wealth of rulers was confronted in divergent ways by *Forbes* and *Fortune* magazines when they both ran cover stories on the world's richest people in October 1987. *Forbes* decided not to include those whose wealth is based on rule, partly because of the difficulty of placing a dollar value on such things as the support provided to dictators (North Korea's Kim Il Sung, for example) by the security organizations under their command. So Japanese property magnate Yoshiaki Tsutsumi was dubbed (as he would be the following year) world's richest, with a worth estimated at more than $21 billion. *Fortune,* on the other hand, considered national wealth to be personal if it was clearly under the control of a ruler. On this basis, Sir Hassanal came out on top with a fortune of $25 billion (a figure which included Brunei's foreign reserves), followed by Saudi Arabia's King Fahd with $20 billion (they were to finish one-two in 1988 as well). Britain's Queen Elizabeth II, with a worth of $7.4 billion, was pegged at fifth richest.

Earlier in 1987, *Time* magazine placed Sir Hassanal's wealth at an even higher level of $30 billion. *Time*'s figure appeared in a short "Business Notes" item focusing on the sultan's recent purchase of a lavishly appointed Boeing 727 jet from a former close business associate, Iran-Contra arms dealer Adnan Khashoggi, who needed some quick cash to prop up his crumbling business empire. Sir Hassanal reportedly "stunned bankers on the scene at his palace" by not delegating the bill-paying task to an accountant, but rather writing out an $18 million check (from an ordinary checkbook in a tattered plastic folder) and then carefully recording its number, date and amount.

That account represents a rare glimpse of how Sir Hassanal operates; he leads a very private life as far as his subjects are concerned. Sir Omar, while he was sultan, cultivated an image of a ruler truly concerned with the welfare of his people, joining them in holiday rowing regattas, tugs-of-war and soccer games and occasionally explaining his policies over the radio. Sir Hassanal joined in public games when he first became sultan but later stopped. Now he seldom appears in public except on important ceremonial occasions. These include observations of his birthday, which falls on July 15. He visits the main town of each of the four districts on different days, and in each place a very British style of parade (now adopted as part of Brunei tradition) is held on a *padang* (grass field). The sultan (in coat and tie or military uniform) and top officials, plus foreign diplomats, arrive in a motorcade and take seats according to rank in a banner-bedecked reviewing stand which they reach by walking along a red carpet. Police and army personnel in ceremonial uniform have already marched onto the field led by a brass band with a bagpipe-playing contingent of Brunei Malays in kilts, and also accompanied by members of such uniformed organizations as the Boy Scouts.

The core of the event involves the sultan being driven in an open Land Rover the hundred or so yards to one end of the uniformed groups lined up facing the reviewing stand. He then walks stiffly up and down the rows followed by a ceremonially attired man holding a yellow umbrella over the sultan's head, and when he has finished his inspection he is taken back to the reviewing stand in the Land Rover with the umbrella still held over his head. The climax is the firing of rifles into the air in salute, and in the capital there is also the flourish of helicopters flying low overhead spewing multi-hued smoke. Until independence, a nearly identical parade was held in the capital on the British queen's birthday (then an official holiday), except that the British high commissioner rather than the sultan would do the inspection (without the accompaniment of an umbrella bearer).

An interesting footnote to the sultan's birthday parades is that umbrellas are traditional insignias of rank among the very upper levels of Bunei nobility. The sultan, the viziers and a few other officials each have their own color (the sultan's yellow was probably adopted from the Chinese emperors of many centuries ago) and on some ceremonial occasions are still accompanied by umbrella bearers. Flags are a more widespread rank sign and were once flown on important occasions even by non-nobles (red and white). Since 1959, however, non-nobles and the lesser nobility are required to fly the Brunei flag. Those still authorized to fly personal standards are listed as: descendants of sultans down to four generations; descendants of viziers down to three generations; descendants of cheterias down to two generations; and certain menteris (non-noble officials).

Returning to the subject of Sir Hassanal's avoidance of the public glare, it has also been noted that most policy announcements are left to lesser officials, and the period between interviews with journalists sometimes stretches for several years. An interview with Newsweek magazine just after independence showed that he follows his father regarding democracy. When asked if free political activity might ever be allowed, he replied: "We have tried it. We had elections before 1962 and we had a few political parties, but people competed against each other and chaos resulted."

Newsweek asked some other challenging questions, such as his reaction to descriptions of him as a high-living playboy. To this he said: "I do enjoy fast cars. But there is no harm in that if you have the money. I'm actually a family man." On criticism of his new Istana as too ostentatious, he countered: "The new palace is a big one. But it was meant to be around for future generations, as a landmark. And Brunei is very wealthy. When a person is rich, he doesn't buy a minicar, he buys a Rolls-Royce."

What the People Think

What do the people of Brunei think of their ruler? It is hard to gauge with any certainty in a land where opinion polls are anathema and there are no channels for the free expression of views. But expatriate residents and visiting journalists who have talked with a cross-section of people seem to agree that most Brunei Malays and to a lesser extent the other indigenous people continue to respect, and to a degree also fear, the office of the sultan. Such feelings have been ingrained for many generations and may be explained as arising from an ancient rationale: give your full allegiance to the ruler and he will protect you with divine support. Even today there are lingering beliefs that the sultan has supernatural powers; many villagers believed Sir Omar could fly right up to the day of his death. So it is no surprise that many Brunei Malays are offended if the sultan is in any way demeaned, or that most young women heed his discouragement of short skirts "because it is our sultan's wish." Neither is there much evidence of envy or discontent over the life of ultimate ease he leads amidst astounding luxury — rather, Bruneians express pride in his grandest of palaces, echoing the official line that it stands as a proud symbol of Brunei itself.

On the other hand, the 1962 rebellion was widely supported by non-nobles. Although the uprising was ostensibly aimed at the colonialist British, emotions against the rigid system of rank among Brunei Malays (which would presumably have been done away with under Azahari's socialism) were undoubtedly an important factor. The current relative lack of political activity makes it hard to say whether many Brunei Malays feel strongly against the system today. But if such feelings do exist, they've been pushed into the background by the spreading of the wealth initiated by Sir Omar largely in response to the rebellion.

One action of Sir Hassanal's which did raise widespread criticism was his taking of a pretty former airline stewardess as his second wife in November 1981 (Islam allows men up to four wives). This was done against the wishes of many royal family members, as shown by the fact that there was only a terse announcement after the fact and no celebrations, in sharp contrast to his first marriage. For many Brunei Malays, especially educated women, the marriage represented a step backward for their country.

The Chinese (the second largest ethnic group), being latecomers to the sultanate, have an entirely different sort of relationship with the powers that be. They have settled in large numbers throughout Southeast Asia and everywhere shown themselves able to adapt to local conditions. They may grumble privately about the all-powerful position of the royal family and lack any respect for the sultan, but they accept the reality of the situation and publicly proclaim their loyalty.

Expatriates are in a similar position, putting aside their true feelings in order to get a piece of the action. Japanese officials involved in major business undertakings have been kept waiting for weeks on end to see His Majesty, and, when the sultan was still a polo fanatic, visiting polo-playing VIPS sometimes went to Jerudong Park at the appointed time for a knockabout only to find it had been abruptly cancelled. The sultanate depends on expatriates to keep both the private and public sectors running, but even the most highly educated and experienced among them can be replaced — so it's possible expulsion for any who offend the sultan or his relatives (sometimes they leave with no idea what they did wrong).

Sir Hassanal's very secrecy about his private life spawns endless speculation and sometimes fanciful tales. Does he really believe he is the reincarnation of the fifth sultan, who also bore the name Bolkiah and who is credited with expanding the last Brunei empire to its greatest extent in the early 1500s? Does he really jet to Bangkok just to womanize? If the sultan engaged in such escapades in the past, their frequency has decreased with a maturation which has been observed by expatriates with long-standing dealings with the royal family. From a distractable young man with little interest in governance, he has become a self-assured ruler who takes his responsibilities as well as his perogatives seriously. He can be moody and quick to anger, though, setting his aides trembling with a sharp glance.

Other Family Members

The passage of Sir Omar left his eldest son clearly in charge, with other male members of the royal family exercising influence approximately proportional to their blood relationship to the sultan. Thus Prince Mohamed ranks second in power. However, Prince Sufri, who as the third eldest brother should come next in terms of power, has apparently had to yield much of it due to his battle with cancer.

Sir Hassanal has six daughters and three sons by his two wives. His heir-apparent is his eldest son (the third child borne by first wife Pengiran Anak Saleha), who was given the name Muhtadee Billah on his birth in January 1974 but is known as Prince Mohamed. Second in line for the throne is Prince Ábdul Ázim, borne by second wife Hajjah Miriam in 1982.

While Sir Hassanal's first marriage was arranged by his parents, his second was romantically rooted. Due to the widespread disapproval of the event, Hajjah Miriam did not begin making regular public appearances until a year or so later. She also stayed in a different palace from the No. 1 wife, with the sultan helicoptering between the two. The wives appeared together in public for the first time during independence celebrations in February 1984, when both sat on the royal dais at the mass rally held at the national stadium.

Brunei's second-in-command, Prince Mohamed, in ceremonial dress.

The private lives of royal family members tend to be as shielded from public view as possible. A rare glimpse into life for royal offspring came in mid-1988 when the *Times* of London ferreted out the information that two former world champion snooker players had been hired to teach eldest son Prince Mohamed the finer points of their sport for more than $5,000 an hour apiece. The lessons were being given in a special snooker room in the sultan's Dorchester Hotel in London and were being professionally videotaped as a further aid to skill development.

A surprising openness to the press was displayed by Prince Sufri in the latter half of 1987 when he was in the regional news for announcing his imminent marriage to Malaysian singing star Muzuin Hamzah. Instead of communicating through spokesmen, he talked freely with reporters and on one occasion showed them a part of his car collection. There was a Ferrari, a Porsche, an Aston Martin and a Maserati with a "talking" camera in the rear which, he explained, let him see who was behind him. He said the couple would live in the old palace, the Istana Darul Hana, as well as in his small mansion called *Villa Cinta Membara* (Villa of Burning Love). Mazuin's family would meanwhile move into his house in the Malaysian capital, Kuala Lumpur; after meeting her, he had named the house *Villa Cinta Bersemi* (Villa of Blossoming Love). It was revealed that nearly $1.5 million was spent on the wedding at the Istana Darul Hana and a similar amount on jewelry for the bride. One might wonder whether Prince Sufri's willingness to give interviews and pose for pictures were in some way related to his general lack of involvement in Brunei's governance.

The sultan's wives, children and brothers clearly share in the wealth — and uncles, aunts, nephews, nieces, cousins and in-laws all enjoy benefits of kinship as well. The traditional posts held by many of the core noblemen have meaning only on ceremonial occasions, but they and their own family members find advancement in the civil service relatively easy and also use their connections to make fortunes in business. Businessmen seeking major government contracts are likely to find the going much easier if they forge connections with royalty. Most leading family members also have their own companies, or are partners in companies, which secure a substantial amount of business from both the government and the Brunei Shell Petroleum Company. The perks of kinship echo the more formal pre–Residency system under which the sultan gave his relatives their own territories or trade monopolies.

The common folk are well aware of the advantages of royal blood ties, and apply an appellation to the beneficiaries which is both humorously ironic and tinged with envy. This is the term *Orang Bukit*, literally "the hill people," which normally denotes natives of the hilly interior who are looked down upon as country bumpkins. The *Orang Bukit* of today's Brunei, however, are the royal family members who have built their palaces and mansions on prime hill tops surrounding the capital.

Royal Family, Inc.

Business seems to have overtaken polo as Sir Hassanal's chief passion. He began pulling some of his vast personal fortune out of staid investment portfolios in August 1983, when he paid an estimated $135 million for Singapore's five-star Holiday Inn (later known as the Royal Holiday Inn) and an adjoining shopping complex. Indeed, this appeared to be the first move in a plan to create an international chain of luxury hotels. He was reportedly interested in Hong Kong's Excelsior until it was withdrawn from the market, and then in early 1985 bought the grand old Dorchester in London, saying he intended to make it the world's most luxurious hotel. A couple of weeks after Sir Omar's death, the newly registered firm of Borneo Properties bought Singapore's Hyatt Regency, across the street from the Royal Holiday Inn, for about $50 million less than the latter even though the Regency is a bigger and grander hotel. The firm's registered directors were a pair of lawyers, but it was widely understood the ultimate owners were royal family members led by the sultan.

Sir Hassanal apparently came to hold hard feelings against Malaysian property tycoon Khoo Teck Puat for selling him the Holiday Inn for what he considered to be an inflated price. As will be described in a later section, the sultan became even angrier when it was discovered that the National Bank of Brunei, managed by Khoo's eldest son and jointly owned by the Khoos and royal family members, had been used to funnel around $650 million in unsecured loans to Khoo family enterprises. After the Hyatt Regency purchase, Sir Hassanal unloaded the Royal Holiday Inn on his government's Brunei Investment Agency, reportedly at no loss, illustrating the tenuousness of the division between government and royalty in the sultanate.

The sultan expanded into the United States in 1987 with the $200 million purchase of the Beverly Hills Hotel, home to famous celebrity watering hole the Polo Lounge. Again, his hand was concealed, with the buyer identified only as Sajahtera, Inc., but the truth was revealed to the business press by sources close to the deal. Sir Hassanal thus joined an ownership list of well-known names. The pink landmark had been owned by the wife of Ivan Boesky, the fallen Wall Street stock speculation wizard, and her family, who sold it in late 1986 to a group headed by Marvin Davis, former owner of Twentieth Century–Fox film studios. This group, however, reportedly came to feel it would cost too much to get the 75-year-old hotel, consisting of 260 rooms and cottages, back into top shape. Enter Sir Hassanal, who can afford to place the desire for penultimate quality ahead of financial considerations.

It is also possible he is the principal owner of another venerable hotel, the Ritz in Paris, despite its owners being listed as the Egyptian (but resident in Britain) brothers Mohamed al Fayed, Salah Fayed and Ali Fayed. Mohamed, well-connected in the Middle East and Britain, became Sir Hassanal's closest business associate in 1984 and was entrusted with power of attorney for certain royal matters, although cracks in the relationship began to appear the following year. At least partially filling a similar role previously had been Mohamed's ultra-rich business enemy, Adnan Khashoggi of Saudi Arabia, who also fell out of favor with the sultan in a short span of time. Khashoggi and Sir Hassanal were later to become well-known figures in the United States' Iran-Contra scandal, the former as a middleman between the United States and Iran and the latter as a major contributor to the Nicaraguan Contras, but apparently there was no connection between their activities in the affair.

It was the Fayed brothers, led by Mohamed, who acted as front men in the Dorchester Hotel purchase. This ploy was apparently intended to keep Sir Hassanal's name out of the negotiations since that could have led to the price being jacked up by the sellers. In any case, he ended up paying nearly $100 million, over twice the price paid when the hotel changed hands about half a year earlier. It was only natural that questions should arise over the ownership of the Ritz, since this classiest of Parisian establishments had earlier been bought by a Fayed company and, in early 1984, Sir Hassanal joined the brothers in instituting the annual $50,000 Ritz Paris Hemingway Award for the English novel best exemplifying the "Hemingway tradition of excellence." On balance, however, the Fayeds do appear to be the Ritz's real owners.

But a far more controversial question of ownership envelops an even bigger Fayed family purchase. There was a great deal of publicity (and shock) in Britain when the brothers concluded an $842 million deal for the House of Fraser, a virtual national institution and retailing giant which owns Harrods, world-famous as the London department store where royalty shops. The move incensed British tycoon Roland "Tiny" Rowland, chief executive of Lonrho, a British conglomerate which had been forestalled in its bid to obtain the House of Fraser for eight years by a government inquiry. Giving the whole affair an appropriately nighttime soap opera atmosphere of tit-for-tat was the fact that Mohamed and Ali Fayed had sat briefly on the Lonrho board of directors in the mid–1970s but resigned, charging that Rowland ran things too autocratically.

In an attempt to head off the Fayeds' House of Fraser deal, Rowland launched a press campaign handled mainly by the newspaper he controls, the *Observer*. One of his main contentions was that the Fayeds lacked the resources to make a purchase of House of Fraser dimensions. He claimed they were merely acting as front men for the real buyer, alleged to be Sir Hassanal, and had failed to give the British government the full details of the deal. When the Hong Kong–based *Far Eastern Economic Review* tried to track down who was really making the purchase, the trail led to Al Fayed Investment and Trust Company S.A., located in Liechtenstein, where further disclosure of other backers could not be obtained.

In any case the British government gave its speedy approval of the purchase in March 1985 after deciding the brothers were, as they claimed, the true owners (the British merchant bank Kleinwort Benson had reported their assets as totalling more than $2 billion in fields ranging from real estate and construction to oil and shipping). But the controversy continued as the London press focused on the timing of the approval, which came less than two months after Mohamed had accompanied Sir Hassanal to a meeting with British prime minister Margaret Thatcher. Not long after the meeting, the sultan shifted large amounts of dollars (reportedly $2 to 3 billion) into sterling in a move widely speculated as designed to prop up the British pound, then at a record low and causing political problems for Thatcher's government. Some commentators saw a connection between this apparent favor on the sultan's part and the House of Fraser purchase approval, but Downing Street and the Fayed brothers denied it, while Sir Hassanal was characteristically mum. Rowland's accusation barrage ended up earning him little else besides a lawsuit for defamation filed against the *Observer* by the Fayeds, although he may have gained some satisfaction at giving the brothers and the sultan much unwanted publicity and quickening the pace of their falling out.

The month after the British government approved the House of Fraser deal, Sir Hassanal relieved Mohamed of his powers of attorney. The last straw was apparently more bad publicity due to actions of Fayed family associates involved in running the Dorchester. They had wanted to terminate the hotel management contract held by Hong Kong–based Regent International, but Regent went to court and the British press was provided with plenty of grist for its mill. "The Sultan feels his name has been dragged through the Fleet Street mud," an acquaintance was quoted as saying by *Newsweek*. And Mohamed al Fayed ended up taking much of the blame.

The House of Fraser affair also featured a number of other colorful characters, including the globe-trotting Hindu religious leader Shri Chandra Swamiji Maharaj. The swami has claimed many among the powerful and rich to be his devotees, including Sir Hassanal, Adnan Khashoggi, Ferdinand and Imelda Marcos, Elizabeth Taylor, John McEnroe and Ryan O'Neal. But there is ample evidence, according to investigative reports in both *New Republic* and *Maclean's* magazines in November 1987, that many of his claims of acquaintanceship are exaggerated, and that his professed interest in the "wealth of the spirit" is outweighed by a concern for the material sort which may have extended (through his Khashoggi connections) to involvement in the Iran-Contra arms transactions of Ronald Reagan's administration. According to Rowland, his rival Mohamed al Fayed gained his introduction to Sir Hassanal by paying the swami $500,000. On the other hand, it has been alleged that Rowland paid the swami more than $5 million for documentary proof of the sultan's involvement in the House of Fraser purchase.

Besides playing the international prestigious property game, Sir Hassanal has apparently been heavily involved in some of the financial markets, notably precious metals. In early 1986, for example, the major gold markets were awash with rumors he had been buying millions of ounces, and this was said to be one of the major factors behind gold's rise to its highest level in 18 months. He is also involved in a variety of Brunei-based enterprises along with his brothers and other relatives. Their investment and holding company, QAF Holdings, in which Prince Mohamed maintains the highest profile, is widely referred to as Royal Family, Inc. It was formed in 1983 to bring under one umbrella close to 20 royal family wholly owned or joint-venture companies involved in shipping, newspaper publishing, food manufacturing and retailing, automotive sales, and Brunei's oil industry. The royal family is also known to control companies incorporated in tax havens elsewhere — for example, Parkwood Investments based in the Channel Islands, which own 60 percent of QAF Holdings. Royal children start amassing their personal fortunes from an early age. The sultan's eldest daughter, Princess Rashidah, was a major shareholder in Brunei's Island Development Bank by the time she was 12.

A number of royal family companies enjoy a privileged position with respect to the local oil industry, which is dominated by Brunei Shell Petroleum, a company half-owned by the Brunei government. There is, for example, Saberu, a royal family joint-venture with Datuk Harris Salleh, the wealthy former chief minister of Sabah. In 1983, this enterprise was reportedly buying a substantial portion of Brunei Shell's crude output (about 30,000 barrels per day, nearly one-sixth of the total) at favorable prices and selling it on to a Japanese trader at a profit.

Then there is the royal family's corporate vehicle, QAF Limited, the name bestowed on Singapore-based Ben and Company (an ailing group involved in retailing, food processing and real estate) following a complex reverse-takeover agreement through which QAF Holdings gained control of Ben from Straits Steamship in 1984. A major advantage for QAF was that it immediately gained a listing on the Singapore Stock Exchange. The exchange requires that companies be in existence for at least five years before listing, so QAF Holdings would otherwise have had to wait until 1988. QAF Limited is also listed on the Kuala Lumpur Stock Exchange.

QAF quickly embarked on the acquisition trail, with the focus on enterprises in the food and retail fields. The company has found, however, that performance, not connections, matters most in the rather unforgiving environment of the business world. Its empire-building efforts proceeded without enough consideration of how the parts would fit together, and at a pace which outstripped the recruitment of capable management. All the "gobbling" led to "indigestion," in the words of one corporate analyst, and a loss of 5.4 million dollars was reported for the year ending March 1987. To help set things right, a few months later business consultant John Richardson was installed as company deputy chairman and chairman of the executive committee. Richardson had formerly headed Hutchison Whampoa, one of Hong Kong's largest and most diversified companies.

The Brunei Malays

The Brunei Malays have much in common with the Malays of Malaysia and Indonesia, sharing Islam as their religion (yet adhering to many pre–Islamic customs), a strong preference for living in coastal areas, and the Malay language. In Brunei their customs and dialect are sufficiently different for them to be considered locally as a distinct ethnic group (the Sarawak Malays share a similar distinction).

They are concentrated, as they always have been, in and around the capital, but are also scattered along other coastal areas of Brunei and nearby parts of Sarawak and Sabah. About one-quarter of the sultanate's Brunei Malays live in Kampong Ayer. Traditionally they were fishermen, traders and craftsmen, but the younger generation has nearly abandoned these occupations to seek (not always successfully) office work.

Stratification

Aside from the core nobility discussed in an earlier section, there is also a large group — close to 10 percent of all Brunei Malays — claiming noble status based on patrilineal descent from one of the sultans. The economic status of these nobles, however, is often no different from Brunei Malay non-nobles because of the emphasis on advancement by merit as promoted by the British. The nobles do enjoy the use of special birth titles followed by their names. Before marriage, male nobles use the title *awangku* and females, *dayangku*; after marriage both sexes use *pengiran* (non-noble females who marry noble males also use *pengiran*).

According to a 1964 government directive, Brunei Malay non-nobles and all members of other groups (except those bestowed with special titles) are referred to as *awang* if male (equivalent to *encik* in Malaysia) and *dayang* if female (equivalent to *cik* or *puan*). *Awang* and *dayang* had been traditionally given by birth to non-nobles of high status. Also important are titles indicating that a Muslim has made the *haj* (pilgrimage to Mecca in Saudi Arabia): *haji* for males and *hajjah* for females. Examples of possible Brunei Malay names are Pengiran Abu Bakar bin Pengiran Haji Metali (*bin* means "son of" and is followed by the father's name) and Dayang Hasnah binte Daud (*binte* means "daughter of" and is followed by the father's name).

There is among many Brunei Malays a feeling of uncertainty over the importance of the traditional rank system in their changing society. This was noted by the American anthropologist D. E. Brown, who wrote in his in-depth study, *Brunei: The Structure and History of a Bornean Malay Sultanate* (published in 1970):

Brunei Malay women preparing mangkuang plant leaves for weaving mats, in Kampong Ayer.

I can see now that my own difficulties in analyzing present-day stratification were but a reflection of the same difficulties experienced by the people of Brunei. Whereas in the past, I presume, one generally knew how to react when rank differences impinged on social situations, today there is uncertainty. In what would seem to be the simplest of social situations — say a housewarming — a multitude of minor quandaries pop up. Should ladies be invited? Should ladies come if invited? Should there be chairs? Should deference be shown to rank? Should the old folks and traditionalists be invited on one night and the young people and modernists on another, or should they be mixed?

Kinship Solidarity

Although *kampong* means village, Kampong Ayer — the quintessential Brunei Malay community — is not a mere village. It consists of about 35 villages each with its own headman, and which are grouped into seven *mukim* each headed by a *penghulu*. The headmen and *penghulus* once had significant powers, such as controlling who could move in and out of their areas, but now simply implement the directives of the government which appointed them.

Many of the villages were traditionally inhabited by people of the same occupation — brassware-makers, fishermen, traders and so on. There were apparently sharp lines drawn, not only between the nobility and non-nobility, but also between groups which practiced different occupations. Skills, implements and property — all of which formed the basis for the economic survival of the occupation group — were passed down from generation to generation. To keep these things "in the family" and out of the hands of strangers, marriage has traditionally been encouraged to relatives, with highest preference often going to first cousins.

Another reason in the past for confining marriages to relatives, or at least to fellow villagers, was that different villages often feuded with each other. Even today many youngsters grow up considering their neighbors to be uncles, aunts, cousins and so on without knowing for sure whether they actually are related by blood.

According to D. E. Brown, Brunei Malay villages closely resemble what anthropologists call the deme, "which may be defined as a local group of people who reckon kinship bilaterally, who require or strongly prefer marriages within the local group, and who are consequently related to each other through intermarriage although exact kinship relationships are not always traceable." Nowadays, however, the divisions between the villages or demes are crumbling, as they have been for decades, because economic specialization has been lost and inter-village marriages have greatly increased.

Whereas marriages were once arranged by the parents, apparently in consultation with the headman, they are now more likely to be in line with the romantic desires of the couples themselves. Marriages between non-nobles and nobles also seem to be increasing in frequency, although matches of non-noble females and noble males are more common than the other way around because the bride-price required to be paid for noble females is generally about twice that for non-nobles.

Muslim law allows men to take up to four wives, but multiple marriages are not common in Brunei and are generally limited to men wealthy enough to afford separate houses for each of their wives (the first seldom consents to sharing her home with any who follow). However, in pre-residency days, many nobles and high-ranking non-nobles kept concubines. Some office-holders had the right to take lower-class girls who caught their fancy, which often led to resentment on the part of those who lost their daughters. Sometimes a high-status man would actually marry someone of low status, but he would send his handkerchief to take part in the marriage ceremony rather than appearing himself.

Wedding ceremonies follow the typical Muslim Malay form, with betrothal ceremonies and wedding feasts marked by the pounding of *hadrah* in the houses of both the bride and groom. The highlight is the

Brunei Malay youths beating hadrah (hand drums) at a Muslim wedding in Kampong Ayer.

bersanding ceremony, which in the past was often the first time the marriage partners laid eyes on each other. In this ceremony, guests "bless" the couple by rubbing some *tepong tawar* (a paste of rice flour and scented water) on their foreheads and the backs of their hands and tossing a few grains of uncooked yellow rice over them from right to left. A wedding feast is normally held at the groom's house, after which he proceeds in grand style to the bride's, accompanied by a merry entourage of friends and relatives; in Kampong Ayer they are likely to travel in a small flotilla of decorated boats. The newlyweds present themselves in the doorway so all in the neighborhood will know their new status, and then the feasting begins again with the men at the front of the house and the women packed into the kitchen and spilling over into the hallway.

Bride-price payments and the now-defunct right of men of the ruling class to "take" concubines reflect the low status of women relative to men in Brunei Malay society. However, the women, like those in most Asian societies, have not shown much eagerness to change the situation.

Newlyweds often move into their own house, but more typically they start off living with the parents of one or the other (but most often of the bride). It is quite common for there to be three or four married couples and three if not four generations under one roof. The modern Brunei Malay house may have Western-style furniture and electric appliances, but is likely to be of traditional symmetrical design: a large living room running the width of the house at the front, a central hallway leading to the rear past two to six bedrooms (one for each married couple and their young children, with any extra ones being taken by older unmarried boys and girls), and a kitchen–work area at the back about the size of the living room.

Brunei Malay men may hold the reins of power and earn the wages, and also enjoy preference under Muslim inheritance law, but all this is balanced to some extent for the women by their control of family matters and especially the strong emotional bonds that are normally developed with their children. This is one reason why young married couples so often live with the parents of one of the partners. There are many advantages to an extended family, including the pooling of resources and helping each other with chores; the grandmother never seems happier than when look-ing after her children's children. If the patriarchal grandfather dies, his role as household head will probably be taken by the eldest married son or possibly a son-in-law. Often a married couple will leave to form their own household after a few years, during which they have saved the necessary resources and had children of their own, and the room they vacate may well be taken by a just-married sibling. The extended family also has its disadvantages, the main one being the large scope for disagreement among so many people — especially in these times of rapid social change, which tends to aggravate conflict between generations.

Entry and Departure

For an illiterate grandmother and her educated daughter or daughter-in-law, one possible source of conflict lies in the wide range of age-old beliefs associated with pregnancy and birth. Many of these beliefs have been virtually forgotten, but expectant Brunei Malay couples are likely to observe at least some of them — just in case — even though a hospital delivery is planned. Among the myriad taboos (many shared with other Borneo peoples) that were once observed by husbands during their wives' pregnancies were not to: wound or kill living creatures (as this could result in defects in the baby at the same places the animal was wounded), or ham-mer nails in the house, shave, plant poles in the ground or fill in a grave (any of which could lead to complications in delivery). The expectant mother also had many taboos to observe, such as one not to lie facing a house pillar. A delay beyond the predicted delivery date was blamed on a *jembalang pontianak* (vampire) sucking the expectant mother's blood.

On delivery, the infant may still these days be rinsed, wrapped in cloth and placed on a tray with the right ear to the west while Koranic verses are recited. The placenta may be placed in a container which is put on a plank to float off to sea. The person who does this must not look back at the plank lest the infant become cross-eyed.

On the third day after birth there is a ceremony featuring offerings and the slaughter of a goat or other animal which is believed will some day carry the newborn's soul to the next world. And on the seventh day there is a ceremony during which the child is named and also shaved bald — although a few hairs may be left on the neck to ward off diarrhea and a few others on the forehead to prevent colds. As well, the eyebrows are sometimes painted with soot from the bottom of cooking pots (the result of cooking over fires fueled by wood or kerosene, now largely replaced by clean-burning liquefied petroleum gas) in order to frighten off evil spirits by giving the impression the tiny babe already has the strength to lift big pots.

According to traditional belief, the mother on delivery should be wiped with medicinal *ubat luta* (water containing salt, saffron and tamarind). However, she is not supposed to bathe until the seventh day, after which her next bath would come on the fortieth day (or, according to some, the forty-fourth). This is one of the prohibitions of *berdiang*, or confinement, which is similar in form to that observed by other Borneo groups as well as the Chinese. The mother was supposed to stay by the fireplace (now probably replaced by a gas cooker) for either 14 or 40 days; the period is now often reduced if it is observed at all.

At the other end of a Brunei Malay's life, the Islamic rites begin with the washing of the body, which is held in the lap of the chief mourner. It is then wrapped in white sheeting, leaving the face uncovered so relatives can kiss the forehead. Burial is done as soon as possible, preferably on the day of death, although this may be delayed to await the arrival of relatives. The body is buried in a coffin in one of the graveyards reserved for Muslims, with the spot characteristically marked by a simple oblong stone standing upright without any inscription.

In cases of violent or accidental death when an autopsy might be called for, Brunei Malay family members commonly refuse permission, believing that "mutilation" of the body, even for medical or legal purposes, is prohibited by the Koran. They also frequently express the feeling that the deceased had already suffered enough without having to "feel" the cuts of a scalpel.

Ancient Beliefs

The Brunei Malays adopted Islam many centuries ago, but the new religion never came close to supplanting a large body of pagan beliefs. Instead, Koranic inscriptions and recitations came to be imbued with magical qualities believed able to keep ghosts away or ensure success in undertakings. During a visit to a Kampong Ayer house, my host, a recent secondary school graduate, pointed out to me a small water-filled, cobweb-encased bottle on a ledge above the door. The bottle had been blessed by an old man skilled at *baca-baca* (reciting spells) and was believed capable of making any thief who entered the house temporarily blind. The young man related a case where just such a magic little bottle was credited with leading to the capture of a thief who was found groping around the house he had broken into, unable to find his way out.

As for black magic, I was assured that Brunei has *bomohs* capable of sending magic *krises* (daggers) far through the night and into the hearts of enemies, just like in Indonesian movies about ancient warriors. But *bomohs* are more commonly called on to cure illnesses or create love potions (the ingredients required may include hair, fingernail clippings, a photograph or unwashed underwear belonging to the target person).

Most *bomohs* can also provide charms against *hantu* (evil spirits) which are commonly blamed for causing accidents, illness and death (but do prove useful to adults who keep children out of mischief with admonitions along the lines of "the *hantu* will get you"). They are believed normally to be invisible, but when they make an appearance they are white with burning red eyes. One should not whistle in the late afternoon or at night as this is said to attract *hantu*. People should also observe customary behavior as failure to do so will leave them, or even other people in the community, spiritually weakened and open to attack by evil spirits. For example, the proper way to decline food that is offered is to touch it with the right index finger, which is then touched to the lips.

Revived Crafts

With regard to old Brunei Malay ways, the government is working to dispel those considered backward while promoting the revival of those felt to be a source of pride. The ancient crafts of silversmithing, *kain songket* weaving and brassware-making, for example, have been rescued from possible oblivion through the establishment of the Brunei Arts and Crafts Center in the mid–1970s to teach the required skills to members of the younger generation. These crafts, with the exception of *kain songket* weaving, were dying out because the offspring of their elderly practitioners were not interested in carrying on the tradition. The center's school, however, has been able to attract students for its two-year courses (which also include wood carving and *songkok*, or Malay hat, making) by offering monthly allowances and helping to market the output of graduates, who get a full 85 percent of the selling price.

The revival of the ancient crafts and the government's commitment to preserving them are underlined by the magnificent 10-story building finished shortly after independence to house the Arts and Crafts Center, located on the right bank of the Brunei River just outside the capital. The center is run by the Brunei Museum, which has its own impressive museum building (exceptionally large for such a small country) a bit farther down the road at Kota Batu. On display are one of Southeast Asia's finer collections of antique ceramics (mainly Chinese) and the largest, most elaborate oil industry exhibit mounted by the Royal Dutch Shell Group anywhere in the world.

One ancient craft which hasn't required government support to continue to thrive is boat-building, as there is still strong demand for wooden boats (now normally outboard-powered) in the 12- to 25-foot range for fishing and use as water taxis. The main boat-building center is, as might be expected, in the part of Kampong Ayer traditionally inhabited by fishermen and now known as Kampong Saba. Blacksmithing, however, is on the verge of disappearing. Kampong Pandai Besi (*pandai besi* means "clever with iron"), in the central part of Kampong Ayer, was once home to dozens of blacksmiths who produced *parang* blades and other items, but by 1984 there was only one elderly part-time practitioner aided by one of his sons. Their mallet strikes are now heard only on Fridays (the Muslim prayer day) and Sundays when the son is off from his salaried government job; they still use the old-fashioned bellows once standard in Borneo, made of a pair of upright hollow logs in which pistons are alternatively thrust up and down by hand.

The "refined" crafts of silversmithing, weaving and brassware-making were traditionally the domain of the people of Kampong Sungai Kedayan (and to a lesser extent a few of the other wards around the mouth of the Kedayan River), and their practitioners were considered aristocrats (the highest non-noble class). According to various legends, the original craftsmen came from overseas. In one version, the first Brunei ruler defeated a Javanese prince in a cock fight, thereby winning a group of Javanese craftsmen. Another version has it that the fifth sultan imported craftsmen from Java and China to work on buildings at the then-capital, Kota Batu, while yet another says the craftsmen are descended from Sumatran royalty.

The British noticed during the 1800s that one group concentrated on making gold and silver items. Because Islam frowns on gold work, they now stick to silver. Their products were once destined mainly for the Brunei Malay nobility, and even today a fair number of silversmiths earn their livings making items for the royal family, but visitors, temporary residents and Brunei Malays with a newfound interest in their roots have also become major customers for silver cups, trays, bowls and Koran holders.

Schoolchildren line up to take water taxis to their homes in Kampong Ayer. Use of such taxis results in continued strong demand for wooden boats.

Kain songket weavers (women all) are kept busy at their hand looms hung in large hardwood frames because the Brunei Malays have retained their love of ceremony. The leading participants at bestowals of titles, investitures and weddings still dress in glittering traditional style, and Brunei *kain songket* (also called *kain bertabor* in the sultanate) is often also the cloth of choice of members of the upper-crust in the rest of the Malay world (where the weaving craft is generally on the wane).

Weaving the cloth requires both skill and endurance. Six yards of fabric with a richly complex pattern to be made into the costume of a high-ranking dignitary usually takes six to eight weeks to weave, although it can be done in a month if the weaver forces herself to work for hours on end. The reward can be substantial, however, with those six yards selling for as much as $1,200. The weaver will of course have to pay for her materials, mainly cotton thread and metallic thread that looks silver or gold although, rarely, thread of Thai silk and real silver will be used.

The background of the cloth is of cotton threads stretched lengthwise in the loom; the standard width is 32 inches or, to put it another way, about 2,400 threads. The metallic threads or sometimes colored ones are woven in crossways to make the complex, standardized patterns, which were previously held entirely in memory but are now sketched out on paper for the new generation of weavers. Their glittering product is tailored into pants, a tunic, a waistband and *dastar* (headgear) for a man's costume, while a woman's consists of a long-sleeved top and a *sarong* (long skirt).

The other major craft being taught at the Arts and Crafts Center is brassware-making, which was a thriving industry with more than 200 practitioners in Kampong Ayer when the first British resident arrived. At that time brass gongs, cannons (often handheld size), lamps and betel nut boxes were still eagerly sought by tribespeople, but fashions began to change after World War II. By the mid-1970s, only seven men, all related by blood, in Kampong Ujung Bukit (at the mouth of the Kedayan River across from Kampong Sungai Kedayan) were still making brasswares, largely for the Istana and government departments. A couple of the elderly experts were recruited to teach at the Arts and Crafts Center, with Haji Ibrahim bin Mohammad Tahir (born around 1910) as chief instructor. His course attracted a total of 18 trainees, including one of his sons, during the first three years, but since then there have been few new ones because the work is considered too hot and hard.

Haji Ibrahim's foundry, on land just behind his above-water house, is the only one remaining in Kampong Ayer, but most brassware-making is now done at the Arts and Crafts Center where a modern gas-fired heater can swiftly take solid hunks of brass to the region of 1,000 degrees Fahrenheit and melt it — a point that used to be reached only after about three hours of stoking a wood fire with the same kind of hollow-log bellows used by blacksmiths. The brass used to be melted in an incredibly resilient thin-walled vessel made only of clay and a few other simple ingredients, but the gas heater has its own metal container.

Aside from the heater, however, traditional tools and methods remain in use. The first step is the making of clay molds to the shape of the inside of the desired object. A layer of wax (mixed with a rubbery tree sap and buffalo fat) is added, over which more clay is placed in layers. On casting day the molds are placed on logs of burning *nyireh* wood to melt the wax, which flows out of an opening left in the clay, and molten brass is then poured in. The heat in the work area gets so intense that the mark of a brassware-maker is the absence of hair on his forearms — it's all been singed off.

Because of revived interest by many Brunei Malays in their heritage, living rooms are commonly decorated with locally made silver and brass items (often intermingled with mementos from trips abroad or such things as wedding photos of Prince Charles and Princess Diana). However, these craft items are seldom felt to be imbued with mystical qualities as many once were. Gone are the days when a man hoped to possess a magical kris or a brass cannon was reverentially handed down from generation to generation along with a descriptive *pantun* (rhyming Malay quatrain). One such *pantun* was recited for me by Haji Ibrahim (with a guffaw at the punch line) about an antique cannon some two-and-a-half feet long:

Kura-kura si-labi-labi,
Anak buaya tenang-tenang.
Singapura si, baru jadi,
Kain sutera champor benang.

Jelarok burong jeladan,
Burong tekukor terbang tinggi.
Dipatut sama dipadan,
Diukor samanya tinggi.

Kinabalu bertingkat pati,
Ambil kumala dimulut naga.
Bila sudah kehendak hati,
Mahal murah dibeli saja.

Like other *pantuns* about cannons, this one describes the creatures ornately cast along the top of the barrel, serving both as decoration and as symbols of its qualities. Its date of manufacture is also indicated by the phrase, "Singapura si, baru jadi" (Singapore has just come into being — around 1820). The *pantun* may be roughly translated as follows:

Tortoise and freshwater turtle,
The crocodile's child is quiet.
Singapore, recently founded,
Silk cloth embroidered with thread.

Jelarok and *jeladan* birds,
The *tekukor* bird flies high.
Fittingly they are matching,
Their tails the same height.

Mount Kinabalu grows more massive,
Snatch the magic gem from the dragon's mouth (at the peak).
If your heart already wants it,
Whether dear or cheap simply buy.

The Kedayans

The second most populous indigenous group after the Brunei Malays are the Kedayans, with whom they are closely associated. They follow the same religion, speak similar dialects of the same language, share a great many customs and appear to be of similar physical stock.

The most obvious difference is occupational, as the Kedayans have traditionally been rice farmers of the coastal plains and low hills. Most of their villages are scattered around the Brunei-Muara District, while in Temburong they are the main ethnic group with about 40 percent of the district's population.

Low Status

The Kedayan proportion of Brunei's population has fallen over the years. A census in 1911 found that Brunei Malays constituted 53 percent of the population and Kedayans 23 percent, while recent figures show Brunei Malays make up 55 percent but the Kedayans only 5 percent. Part of the explanation is that many Kedayans have been assimilated as Brunei Malays through intermarriage or other means — an attractive shift because even most non-noble Brunei Malays have always enjoyed higher status.

The reason for that difference in status lies in the age-old consideration of the Kedayans as a subject people of the sultan who functioned to provide the Brunei Malays with rice in exchange for cloth, pots and other goods. In the past, Kedayan sons also fought under Brunei Malay nobles. By living near the capital under the protection of the sultan, the Kedayans enjoyed more peaceful farming conditions than most other parts of Borneo.

According to local legend, the first Kedayans were brought from Java by Sultan Bolkiah about five centuries ago to cultivate wet rice. Another account, which seems more likely, is that they are the descendants of Muruts — a pagan, rice-farming people of northeast Borneo — who adopted Islam and allied themselves with the sultan. A similar explanation of Murut origin has been advanced for the Brunei Malay sub-group known as the *puak sakai*, the main inhabitants of Kampong Ayer's once-great fishing villages. Like the Kedayans, the *puak sakai* are of low status and are eligible to fill only the lowest traditional offices. Interestingly, the Kedayans and *puak sakai* together were the providers of what were, and to a large extent still are, the staples of the Brunei diet — rice and seafood.

Like other Borneans, many Kedayans still believe in the possibility of black magic and may blame illness or death on suspected practitioners of the craft. They are believed to obtain the help of a spirit known as *hantu rangau*. In one rite, after reciting a secret spell, the magician stabs the ground with a knife which supposedly leads to the death of the intended victim unless he or she has a *hantu rantau* for protection.

The Farming Life

Kedayan life revolves around the land. Previously, ownership of a plot of land was established by being the first to clear it of jungle, but now of course titles issued by the government are required. In any case there is no longer much pressure for the opening of jungle areas because the number of farmers is dropping. Elderly Kedayans still devote themselves to the planting-harvest cycle almost to their last breath, but most members of the younger generation prefer salaried jobs. They do, however, retain strong ties to the land and on their days off may help with planting, weeding and, above all, harvesting.

As among the Brunei Malays, marriage is encouraged between cousins in order to keep property, especially all-important land, in the family. The land most highly valued is that suitable for growing rice, low-lying and away from rivers and estuaries. Other land is used for growing fruits and vegetables or, on slopes, dry rice.

Water buffalo (*kerbau*) are often grazed on communal land. In contrast to many other parts of Southeast Asia where water buffalo are kept, these beasts in Brunei and nearby parts of Borneo are valued more as symbols of wealth than the work they are capable of doing. Although they may be used occasionally to pull a plow through a rice field, they generally spend their lives grazing and awaiting slaughter at a wedding or other feast.

Most Borneo peoples live in villages consisting of houses clustered tightly together or of a single longhouse in which residents stay under one roof. Kedayan houses, however, tend to be in small clusters or even isolated singly, close to the fields, gardens and orchards; fruit trees serve to mark land boundaries. Perhaps the Kedayans in the past were able to adopt such a housing arrangement because living close to the sultan meant they were relatively safe from marauding pirates and headhunting tribes (the longhouse way of life, grouping people close together, is widely considered to have evolved for defensive purposes).

The agricultural year starts in June or July when the rice fields are cleared of weeds and old rice stems with machete-like *parangs*. The right time to carry out this work was traditionally determined by the appearance of the constellation known locally as "The Seven Stars" (the Pleiades) over the horizon near dawn. In normal years this is followed by a couple of relatively dry months (July and August) during which the cleared vegetation dries out for firing. In the meantime, a nursery is started on a nearby slope. The seedlings are transplanted four to six weeks later, shortly after the field has been fired; plowing or other intensive preparation of the land, aside from repairs to water-holding bunds, is generally not done. The Kedayans seldom irrigate their fields but rely on rain catchment (the wettest months of the year tend to be from October to January).

The fields are weeded regularly until the rice grains start to appear, after which efforts are switched to keeping pests at bay. Rats, insects and, in remoter areas, monkeys, deer and wild boar can all do serious damage, but the most feared pests are flocks of small sparrows called *burong pipit*. To combat this scourge, scarecrows and bamboo noisemakers (such as a windmill-like contraption that makes an eerie whirring sound) are set around the fields. In addition, a small hut on stilts is built in the middle of each field, from which strings hung with pieces of bright cloth or plastic as well as bamboo clappers radiate in all directions. At least one family member must be on duty during daylight hours in this "control central" to yank on the strings in parts of the field where sparrows settle. They are temporarily scared off but inevitably try an attack elsewhere.

There's a palpable feeling of excitement in a Kedayan village at harvest time, which usually falls in March or early April but can be as late as May. If you walk into a rice field during the harvest, two sounds will be heard to continually drift through the air — the *cheep-cheep-cheep* of sparrows and the chatter and laughter of groups of Kedayan women moving waist-deep through the stalks as they cut the heavy brown pannicles with hand knives and put them in baskets at their waists. There will also be occasional sharp shouts by the guardians — generally women or boys — against the sparrows as they pull on the bird-scaring strings or patrol the edges of the fields with long bamboo poles or palm fronds. Groups of families cooperate during the harvest (and in other field work as well), with the women harvesting each field in turn and the men carrying the grain in big rattan or palm leaf baskets to storage huts. These huts are a unique part of Kedayan villages as other farming groups in this region of Borneo generally store their rice in their houses. The huts are raised on stilts with discs part way up to keep out rats, and nowadays the structures almosts always have corrugated zinc roofs, but the walls are made of traditional materials such as split bamboo and bark.

Most Kedayans still celebrate the harvest festival called *Makan Tahun* (annual feast). This in the past was apparently a much more elaborate affair than presently observed, mainly because it was based on ancient pre-Islamic spiritual beliefs which are now strongly frowned upon by Brunei's religious authorities. In its traditional form, the feast provided offerings to various gods to express thanks for the harvest and to gain their blessings for the next planting cycle. It also served to honor the dead, who were believed actually to attend the feast, thus ensuring the spiritual unity of all family members whether living or departed. In fact, many Kedayans still hold what they call *Makan Arwah* annually in remembrance of a departed relative. This feast is similar to *Makan Tahun* but is held on a smaller scale at any time of the year.

Often in the past a village's *Makan Tahun* was sponsored by a single individual seeking to raise his prestige, at the risk of ridicule if the food and drinks were not enough to satisfy all the guests. Now the feast is almost always a cooperative affair with each family contributing money and provisions, and with the feast plates and glasses owned communally, although individuals may still gain prestige by contributing such things as a buffalo for slaughter. Preparations include the building by the men of a temporary dining hall about 10 feet wide and, depending on the number of guests expected, between about 80 and 350 feet long, plus sheds for cooking and shelter for the women and children (the dining hall is a male preserve). The feast used to last seven days or so, but now it is normally only three: assembling provisions on the first day, cooking on the second and eating with the guests on the third. The second afternoon is marked by music, dancing and games by the men to prevent boredom among the workers. Then around 9 P.M. men of high religious standing, such as Imams (congregation leaders) and Hajis, begin a night-long procession, slowly circling inside the village men's hall while rhythmically chanting Arabic words. This is *ratib saman*, which may have been derived from an all-night pre–Islamic ceremony inviting the gods and ancestral spirits to the feast.

On the feast day itself, the guests normally start arriving shortly before noon and are served rice and various accompanying dishes as they take their seats in opposite rows on mats on the ground, or, more commonly now, in chairs at long tables. When they leave, they are given some *kelupis*, a kind of rice cake which is the central food of the feast.

Top-spinning contests were once an eagerly awaited part of the festivities, as they served to express inter-village rivalries. Such contests are now, however, seldom held because most younger Kedayan men are not interested in gaining the skills needed to make and use the big, heavy hardwood tops. Whereas competing teams were once expected to have 40 or so members each, today only 15 or 20 are likely to be recruited. The sport is an ancient one which apparently reached Brunei from the Malay Peninsula; an epic top-spinning contest is recounted in the *Shaer Awang Semaun* between two mythic characters (one of whom wielded a top as big as a mountain) who lived at the time of Brunei's first Muslim sultan.

Among the Kedayans, top-spinning is not a children's game but a serious affair with spiritual overtones for the adults, for according to traditional belief, success at the sport during *Makan Tahun* helps to ensure a good rice harvest the following year.

There are several top-spinning games, the most popular involving members of opposing teams hurling their tops to the ground in turn and trying to knock down an opponent's top. Tops which come through standing are scooped up by their throwers on the blades of small wooden paddles, and the top spinning the longest is the winner. But it can take quite a while to determine the outcome — up to 45 minutes, for that is how long the larger tops can keep spinning. These are about 30 inches in diameter and weigh about 8 pounds. Tops of similar size but made nearly twice as heavy through the addition of tin can spin for up to an hour and 40 minutes; these

Preparing to hurl a large wooden top in a beach fair contest — top spinning is an ancient sport among the coastal peoples of the Malay Archipelago.

are so difficult to make properly that only team leaders are likely to have them. These days, easier-to-make smaller tops six to eight inches in diameter are seen most often, and they normally keep spinning only 15 to 20 minutes. An indication that top-spinning has lost its religious significance is that tops may be used for years, in contrast to the old custom of making new tops while carefully observing various taboos before each *Makan Tahun*.

Other Indigenes

Like the Kedayans, Brunei's other indigenous peoples have to a large extent been absorbed and obscured by more dominant groups. Early in this century their numbers as a whole were comparable to the Kedayans as they constituted about one-fifth of the population; today they remain roughly equivalent to the Kedayans, that is at little more than 5 percent. A main reason, again, is intermarriage, with Brunei Malays and Kedayans as well as Chinese, Ibans and other immigrants.

Although the indigenes have generally lived their lives according to their own traditions and inclinations, they have recognized the authority of the sultan for centuries. They have been loosely incorporated into the

Brunei Malay stratified scheme of things through the bestowal by the sultan of titles on their leaders. These "land chiefs" rank just below those of the Kedayans and are addressed as either *Dato* or *Orang Kaya.*

The Bisayas

The British early on recorded that the interior areas of the Tutong and Belait districts were inhabited by a variety of tribal groups including the Tutongs, Belaits, Dusuns and Bukits. Although none of these groups have been studied in any depth, it is known that they are actually the same people because they speak dialects of the same language and have similar customs. These people are also found in Sarawak (especially in Limbang) where they are called Bisayas, which can be considered a more appropriate term than the others because Tutong and Belait simply refer to the rivers along which those particular groups live, while Dusun and Bukit are terms also used elsewhere in Borneo to denote "people of the hills" (that is, inhabiting inter-riverine areas and being great walkers rather than boat users).

The Bisayas are believed to have settled in the area in very ancient times; they have no origin myths of having migrated from anywhere else. Like most other pagan Borneo peoples, their traditional religious beliefs included descent from demi-gods and the reception of messages from the spirit world via omen birds. But unlike some other groups, the Bisayas (or at least the Bukit sub-group) favored neither elaborate body tattoos nor heavy earrings capable of stretching the lobes down to the shoulders. They did file short their teeth and permanently blacken them with the gum of a jungle tree.

The Bisaya sub-groups followed the tribal Borneo way by generally regarding outsiders as enemies, whether or not they spoke the same language. Inter-tribal warfare was once rife and warriors sought to prove themselves by taking enemy heads, possession of which was believed to yield some of the victims' spiritual power to the new owners. Main enemies to the west included the Kayans and Kenyahs of the Baram River system who pushed many of the Metings to the Belait where they were accepted by and intermingled with the Bisayas. It appears that Brunei's Bisayas were once quite numerous but suffered a severe decline, perhaps due to epidemics of smallpox and other diseases, some time before the British residents arrived and introduced census-taking.

Traditional Bisaya ways have since been largely discarded and Christianity or Islam adopted (the Tutongs as a group were Islamicized a great many years ago). Many old customs do linger, especially among those of the older generation who never went to school and still grow hill rice the

These relics of headhunting days, obtained by Bisaya men, lie in a shed (protected from curious tourists by wire mesh) next to the Belait River.

ancient slash-and-burn way or, in some sub-coastal areas, process sago palm as their staple food. Kuala Balai, about 20 miles up the Belait River, remains a sago-processing center. Although the villagers have become Muslim, they still hold occasional ceremonies to appease the spirits believed associated with a collection of skulls from headhunting days which are kept in a small riverside shelter (now screened over the open front to prevent disturbance by curious visitors).

Ceremonies still observed by the Dusun sub-group include various dances (*alai*) accompanied by offerings through which the gods (of whom "Awang" is chief) are contacted to remove taboos from food. Immediately after the rice harvest, the *alai padi* is performed along with the offering of rice, eggs, bananas and rice cakes on seven trays, because it is believed that otherwise blindness, or possibly death, will result when the newly harvested rice is eaten. The dance itself involves a night-long procession around a huge pile of uncooked rice in the shape of a crocodile, which is covered with slices of copra representing scales. The dance culminates near dawn with the "killing of the crocodile" ceremony in which the rice pile is slashed with sago palm "knives." Village elders then slice in half a live chicken and pluck out the heart to be eaten, yellow rice is sprinkled around — and the taboos on eating the new rice are believed dispelled. Later in the year another *alai* is performed to remove taboos on stored unhusked rice, while still other *alai* are done as frequently as once a month to banish taboos on other foods, including eggs, rice cakes and fruits.

The customary burial practices of the Bisayas have also endured to some extent even among those who have adopted one of the world's major religions. An essential feature which is shared with many other indigenous groups is the placing of objects on the grave for the use of the departed in the next life; the site is sheltered by a small open wooden hut. Although this sort of burial has ancient roots, it has been brought into line with the changing times. The hut is likely to be roofed with corrugated zinc, and underneath there will almost certainly not be such hand-fashioned things as earthenware cooking pots, spears and cloth of traditional weave, as there used to be. Rather, there will be mainly machine-made items — tin plates, glass cups, metal cooking pots and store-bought shirts on wire hangers. When I visited a hill-top Bisaya graveyard in the Tutong District, I spotted some rather interesting items which had obviously been highly valued by their now-departed owners. On one woman's grave there is a rusting foot-operated sewing machine, while hanging from another wooden shelter is a run-down wall clock. Most of the grave-top objects there are of relatively little value, but there is a notable exception — a scrambler-type motorcycle with relatively low mileage. This was the treasured possession of a young man who had been in the armed forces and drowned in a boating accident around 1980.

The Penans

While various Brunei Malay nobles once considered certain Bisaya sub-groups as "theirs" to trade with and tax, some Bisaya leaders in turn "owned" groups of nomadic Penans for trading purposes. As the Penans wandered the deep, rugged interior clad in bark loincoths, they would collect jungle produce such as hornbill feathers and bezoar stones to trade for iron knife blades and tobacco. The Bisayas would then trade the jungle produce on at great profit, and it would eventually be sent overseas through the Water City bringing in tremendously greater profits.

The staple food of the nomads was sago from smaller species of the palm than that of the sub-coastal swamps. Penan bands would stay in temporary huts of saplings and leaves bound together with rattan and move on when the sago in the area dwindled. The men also hunted with blowpipes, and wild-growing fruits and vegetables were also part of the diet; an alcoholic beverage was brewed from a fruit called *buah tampoi*.

Brunei's few remaining Penans have, however, adopted a settled way of life, although the call of the jungle still has an obvious hold on them. A band of 21 decided to try settled life at Sukang, far up the Belait River, in

A Penan man (formerly nomadic, now settled) boring a hole in a thick pole which will be shaved down into a blowpipe. Blowpipes are still in demand for hunting since the possession of firearms is forbidden in Brunei.

1963, and they were later joined by the remaining 15 nomads. Twenty years later there were 45 of them living in a longhouse of 8 contiguous rooms (one for each family) which was built for them by the District Office with timber donated by Chinese-owned sawmills.

Today they are agriculturists, growing both wet and hill rice (but still almost no vegetables) as well as *rembia*, the large sago palm of the swamps, and occasionally drinking rice wine. The men still set off to hunt for days at a time — alone except for a few small hunting dogs — with blowpipes and darts tipped with the poisonous sap of jungle trees. Blowpipes, in fact, are one of the few sources of cash income for the Penans as they are in demand by the tourists and British army and Gurkha men who trickle through. Other villagers in the area also buy or trade for Penan blowpipes for hunting because the shotguns they would prefer to use have been banned since the abortive 1962 revolt.

It takes a Penan man about a week of on-and-off work to fashion a blowpipe, normally about six feet long, out of a certain kind of hardwood which is disappearing, along with the game, in the nearby jungle. To bore a hole straight down the middle of a hardwood cylinder about three inches in diameter, the borer squats on a raised sapling platform from which the cylinder is suspended and spins a long iron rod with a sharp tip between his palms. Every now and then he stops boring to pour water into the lengthening hole and float out the wood shavings. When the hole is finished he shaves the cylinder down to a diameter of about one inch and attaches an iron spearhead, obtained from an Iban blacksmith, to the end.

Compared to the longhouses of other indigenes, the Penan dwelling seems austere and empty, for it was never their custom to collect various items as heirloom symbols of wealth and prestige. After all, it would have been quite impractical for the nomads to lug big Chinese jars, Brunei brasswares and human skulls on their wanderings. Their nomadic way of life naturally made them very different from settled peoples in other ways. They don't celebrate any big festivals but have only small, rather informal ceremonies. When somebody died, they simply left the body in a hut and moved on (although they now bury their dead). They were never headhunters — a practice apparently related to inter-tribal competition for the best farming land — but avoided armed conflict. Neither did the Penans build up a body of oral literature, probably because the wandering bands did not meet often enough to pass on and keep alive legends and genealogies. As a result of their unique nomadic past, the integration of the Sukang Penans into Brunei's coalescing indigenous society has been extremely slow. As of 1983 there had been only two intermarriages (to Bisayas) and both had ended in divorce, and only one young man had ventured to the coast in search of wage-paying work.

The Muruts

The Muruts are another group which has been giving up its own unique religion for Islam or Christianity. There are only a few hundred of them in Brunei, in the Temburong District, where they live mainly in longhouses on the upper reaches of the Temburong River. Despite their relative insignificance now, the Muruts once played an important role as providers of military muscle for the sultan. Most resided in Limbang, which separates

Temburong from the main part of Brunei, but as recounted earlier, over-bearing Brunei rule led to a revolt late in the nineteenth century and annex-ation by Sarawak. Like the Bisayas, the Muruts have a headhunting past and grow mainly hill rice, besides being keen hunters and riverine fishermen.

The Ibans

The Ibans are by far Brunei's most vigorous native group, with numbers rising rather than declining. They began filtering into the sultanate from Sarawak around 1900 and have since come to put considerable ter-ritorial and cultural pressure on the Bisayas and Muruts, many of whom have been absorbed into the Iban community through intermarriage.

The Ibans are widely considered to have been Borneo's most successful headhunters, not because they were well-organized militarily (they weren't) but because most Iban men were highly motivated to prove themselves and increase their spiritual power by taking enemy heads. They began entering the western end of present-day Sarawak about three centuries ago, virtually exterminating some of the smaller groups and pushing the powerful Kayans and Kenyahs to the east. Although the Ibans customarily lived on the upper reaches of rivers where they grew hill rice, many in Sarawak pushed down to the coast where they learned to grow wet rice, and some warriors joined up with Malay pirates — the Malays after booty and the Ibans in search of heads on the high seas. These were among the first Ibans encountered by the Europeans, so early on they were called Sea Dayaks.

With the ending of headhunting early in the 1900s, largely through the efforts of the White Rajahs, Iban men began putting more energy into the old custom called *bejalai* (to journey) to satisfy their wanderlust and prove themselves. *Bejalai* used to denote making expeditions lasting up to several months in search of valuable jungle produce, but for many decades Iban men have also sought their fortunes by taking wage-paying jobs. They used to return home with such symbols of success as Chinese ceramics or brass gongs; nowadays the items of choice are likely to be outboard motors, chainsaws and television sets. Brunei has been one of the prime destinations for men on *bejalai* ever since the oil industry sprang up with its high demand for labor. Instead of returning to Sarawak, many of the Ibans stayed, settling down to farm; their longhouses are found mainly on the Belait and Temburong rivers and in the Labi area. Of the earlier settlers, many came to be considered subjects of the sultan, but this status is not easily gained by more recent migrants, who often arrive and stay illegally. The main illegal entry point is the disused Pagalan Canal connecting the Baram and Belait rivers where they come within about two miles of each other. Jungle tracks in this area are also used.

Like the Kedayans, the Ibans relied on the appearance of the Pleiades to indicate the start of the rice planting season in the days before calendars. Their slash-and-burn system of growing hill rice is similar to that of other groups, including the Bisayas and Muruts. A plot of jungle is cleared (the first family doing so having established ownership) and the vegetation allowed to dry out to be burned off, usually in August, which has such beneficial effects as destroying weeds and insect pests and providing nutrient-rich ash. The land is not tilled (which would only loosen the soil and allow it to be washed off the slope by rain), but the seeds are planted directly in holes poked with dibbling sticks, normally in September. There is a mid-season weeding and then the harvest in February or March. A plot is planted for only one or two years, after which it is allowed to lie fallow to regain fertility — hence the land-hungry nature of Borneo's interior tribes. The fallow period is ideally on the order of 12 or more years, but population pressures in most areas have led to shorter periods.

The Ibans are relatively stronger adherents to their traditions than most other indigenous groups, and this trait has led in Brunei to their absorption of many neighboring Bisayas and Muruts rather than the other way around. Even Iban converts to Christianity or Islam tend to continue observing many of the rituals of their traditional religion, which is essentially a rice cult aimed at ensuring ample supplies of their staple food. Like other rice-planters of the interior, they celebrate a harvest festival believed to be attended by gods, mythical heroes and the spirits of ancestors who are feasted and given offerings in thanks, and asked in prayers for help for the next planting cycle. A pig is sacrificed at the climax and its liver examined by knowledgeable elders, who can judge by its shape and markings whether the future holds good or ill. If prospects look bad, more offerings will have to be made to satisfy the gods, who signal their acceptance through the healthy appearance of the liver of the next pig to be sacrificed.

The Chinese

Although many thousands of Ibans have come and often gone, their overall impact on Brunei has not been great because they fill lower niches in the workforce and tend to settle away from the main population centers. Such has not been the case with the Chinese, who dominate the sultanate's commercial sector (which has developed mainly due to their efforts), and who also comprise a large proportion of the technicians and managers. Because of their economic success, they tend to be even better off than the Brunei Malays in terms of ownership of cars, appliances and electronic gadgets.

Most of the original Chinese migrants were dirt poor and came to

The main street (lined with Chinese-run shops) in Kuala Belait, Brunei's second largest town.

Brunei to escape economic hardship in their motherland, to which they had every intention of returning once they had made their hoped-for fortune. The Communist takeover of China more or less ended that dream, and also resulted in an influx of new migrants via Hong Kong. Other Chinese have also arrived from Sabah, Sarawak and the Peninsula in search of better job or business opportunities. The main dialect groups are the Hakka, Hokkien and Teochew.

Like most immigrant groups anywhere, the Chinese in Brunei have tended to stick together. Under the British they were allowed to establish their own schools, many of which still exist but are required to follow the same basic curriculum as government and other private schools. Indeed, the high value they generally place on education is a major reason they have outstripped indigenous peoples in the technical and commercial fields. As a group, they have also been observed to be extremely hard-working and frugal, although some members of the younger generation who have never known hardship display opposite traits.

It is also mainly the older generation that keeps alive various Taoist-Buddhist traditions. Almost every Chinese house and shop (even auto workshops and furniture factories) has a small red wooden altar where offerings of oranges and lighted joss sticks are placed daily. Each main town has a Chinese temple with a resident god who can be asked for favors or consulted on the future, including the suitability of prospective marriage partners. There are also Chinese graveyards with their characteristic above-ground burial vaults. Offerings honoring the ancestors are placed at the graves and the surrounding area cleaned up by relatives on certain Chinese festival days. Chinese New Year is the main annual celebration, during which Brunei's commercial life comes to a virtual standstill for two or three days. Chinese traditions are, however, slowly disappearing, a process hastened by the adoption of Christianity by a large percentage of the immigrants, or of Islam by a much smaller percentage.

Although most of the Chinese have been long resident in Brunei, fewer than 10 percent have been granted citizenship. Many have satisfied the requirement of residency for 20 out of the previous 25 years, but fail to pass a Malay language test which they claim is administered in a way meant to keep them in the limbo of non-citizenship of any country. The main stumbling block is a section on general knowledge of Brunei in which they may be required to recite facts about local flora and fauna so obscure that even most educated Brunei Malays would fail.

During the protectorate period, the Chinese and a handful of Indians and other non-citizens were at least issued with British-protected passports. As independence approached, the British pressed Sir Hassanal and Sir Omar to solve their so-called "Chinese problem" by granting citizenship on a wide scale. That this advice would not be heeded became clear shortly before independence when the government stressed to the Brunei Chinese Chamber of Commerce (the closest thing to a body representing Chinese interests) that the Chinese and other immigrants would have to adapt themselves to life in an Islamic Malay sultanate (and prove it by passing that onerous Malay language test) if they wanted to be accepted. Reasons for maintaining the status quo probably included the fear that the Chinese as citizens could more easily become a potent political force (as in Malaysia), and also the desire not to alienate the Brunei Malay power base, which was already somewhat envious of Chinese business success and wealth.

And so the arrival of independence was a time of apprehension for most of the Chinese, as it meant they became stateless. They can still travel overseas, on Brunei-issued international certificates of identity, but each departure requires a supplicatory application to the government bureaucracy which can take two or more weeks to be approved. Of course, returning to Brunei isn't quite like coming home—which is a natural stimulus for thinking of not returning at all. It has even been speculated that the government has an unannounced policy of making Chinese residents feel unwelcome to encourage their emigration and so reduce their numbers to a more manageable level. Whether this is the government's intention or not, Chinese emigration has been substantial in recent years. Canada was the most popular destination until the mid-1980s when Australia gained that distinction after introducing a liberal new migrants policy aimed at luring skilled people to fill a wide range of professional and technical jobs. So many Brunei Chinese (mostly non-citizen oil industry employees) rushed to apply that Brunei overtook London, at least temporarily, as Australia's fourth biggest migrant post. Australia's business migrants program initially attracted about 30 wealthy Brunei Chinese entrepreneurs who pledged to invest a total of more than $A32* million in return for the rapid granting of citizenship for themselves and their families.

*Australian dollars

V
Abode of Peace – and Prosperity

Brunei today enjoys peace and prosperity. Most people have never had it better economically, although many grumble privately, perhaps about the fact they can't freely express themselves, or about the slowness of the bureaucracy to deal with some problem. But virtually nobody is willing to rock the boat.

There is therefore no need for the sultan to keep the power at his disposal on display. Soldiers do not roam the streets, and even the police keep a low profile. Yet the atmosphere is often pervaded by uneasiness and suspicion and people dare not talk too openly. "You never know who you're talking to," one Brunei Malay explains. "He might go back and report you." To whom? To one's department head, to the police's Special Branch, to some shadowy internal security organization.... Suspicious-looking mail, both incoming and outgoing, is routinely opened, and there are rumors of widespread telephone tapping. But there's little fear of being locked up; people mainly worry about their livelihoods. A civil servant may lose any chance for promotion, a Chinese contractor may fail to get any business, an expatriate worker may be given 24 hours to leave the country. The controls are subtle, and effective.

Islam is another pervasive fact of life in Brunei. While there is freedom of worship and at least 40 percent of the populace is non–Muslim, Islam takes precedence as the official religion. Its status is reflected in the large size and significant influence of the Religious Affairs Department (devoted solely to Islam), the virtual lack of nightlife due to restrictive municipal regulations, vocal diplomatic support of the Palestinian Liberation Organization, and an unannounced policy of refusing to grant work permits to any foreigners known to be Jewish. Although some members of the royal family are rumored to indulge in distinctly non–Islamic carryings-on when traveling overseas, at home they come across as devout Muslims. The promotion of Islam, however, appears to have rather less of a devotional and more of a political impulse, functioning to keep the minds of the common folks focused elsewhere besides dissent.

112

The following sections are intended to give a fuller socioeconomic picture of Brunei.

A One-Track Economy

In 1984, World Bank figures showed that Brunei was the world's second wealthiest country in per capita terms with annual earnings of $22,150 per person, behind only the United Arab Emirates ($24,080) but barely ahead of Qatar ($22,070). And by the end of that year, thanks to oil and gas, its foreign reserves stood at an enviably massive $14-plus billion. Per capita income fell as the 1980s progressed due to declining oil prices, yet foreign reserves headed towards $25 billion thanks to continuing budget surpluses and substantial investment income.

When discussing Brunei's economy, there is little to talk about aside from the petroleum industry. Oil and gas account for 99 percent of the value of exports and about 70 percent of gross domestic product. The output comes entirely from the Brunei Shell Petroleum Company (BSP), which during the early 1980s was providing the Royal Dutch Shell Group with an estimated 20 percent of its worldwide profits. The group owns half of BSP while the Brunei government owns the other half. However, the government retains about 85 percent of the profits through royalties and taxes, allowing it to pamper the populace in what has been dubbed "the Shellfare state." The BSP's predominant role in the economy is clearly shown by the fact that its annual budget rivals that of the government (the company announced a budget of about $1.1 billion for 1984 compared to the government's $1.25 billion).

Oil companies were drawn to the sultanate starting in the 1890s by the presence of oil seepages, and this strong indication of viable deposits was probably among British considerations in agreeing to take Brunei fully under wing in 1906. A number of exploratory wells were drilled, but only the Shell Group's British Malayan Petroleum Company finally made a commercial strike, in 1929, at the western end of Brunei. The Seria oilfield turned out to be about eight miles long and a mile and a half wide, partly under the sea but mostly under the flat, swampy coastal plain. The heavily jungled area teemed with wild boar, crab-eating macaque monkeys, malaria-carrying mosquitoes and crocodiles. The development of the oilfield and the growth of the twin oil towns of Seria and Kuala Belait pushed the boar and most of the monkeys into the interior, although crocodiles remained so common into the late 1950s that BSP — which was created in 1957 during a reorganization of British Malayan Petroleum — hired professional crocodile hunters. These included a Mat Yassin bin Hussin who, at the age of 62, claimed to have caught 700 of them.

It was, however, the swampy land that proved most troublesome in the development of the oilfield. Millions of tons of sand had to be used as fill so drilling and production could proceed on a firm footing. But even then the area's high water table led to frequent flooding, especially during the annual monsoon, and king tides would periodically push the South China Sea far inland. The BSP had to build a long dike along the seafront to keep out the waters, which could topple drilling rigs and damage wellheads by washing the soil from around their foundations.

By the early 1950s, the natural pressure which brought oil to the surface was falling and so "nodding donkey" oil pumps were introduced. Now these green-painted creatures dot the flat landscape around the prosperous town of Seria, their heads monotonously rising and falling in front of the mosque, between the green-roofed and white-walled BSP company quarters, along the beach, beside a Shell gas station, among huge oil storage tanks, and behind the small airport used by helicopters servicing the offshore oilfields.

Oil production offshore began in the mid–1960s and came to greatly outweigh the declining production on land; within 20 years, more than 200 offshore structures were in operation. Of great significance was the discovery of large deposits of associated natural gas which is used as feedstock for Asia's first major (and what was once the world's largest) liquefied natural gas (LNG) plant. The five-train Lumut plant is owned and operated by Brunei LNG, in which the Brunei government, Royal Dutch Shell and Japan's Mitsubishi Corporation are partners. Gas is supplied by BSP from its Southwest Ampa field 24 miles away, liquefied, and sold by Brunei LNG to Brunei Coldgas (owned equally by the same three partners) which charters seven special LNG tankers from Shell Tankers (U.K.) to make deliveries to Japan.

The LNG is used as fuel by three Japanese utilities under a 20-year supply contract with ends in 1993. The contract calls for a minimum of 155 cargoes a year (more than five million tons, derived from 900 million cubic feet of natural gas) which during the early 1980s represented nearly one-third of Japan's LNG imports.

As for other petroleum producers, Brunei's oil revenues shot up after the 1973 worldwide oil squeeze and LNG exports were initially far behind crude oil in value. Later, however, crude prices stabilized and even fell, while those for LNG increased, and by the early 1980s LNG sales brought in about 40 percent of export earnings. A few years later this percentage grew even further as crude prices tumbled. However, competition from new LNG plants in Sarawak, Indonesia, Australia and elsewhere make it unlikely that Brunei will be able to negotiate a new supply contract as favorable as its first one, especially since the Japanese buyers found LNG to be a more expensive fuel than crude oil.

"Nodding donkey" oil pump in front of the mosque in the town of Seria.

The BSP's biggest field, discovered offshore in 1970, is appropriately named Champion. Centrally located in the field, in about 110 feet of water 75 miles northwest of Seria, is a huge complex of 12 interconnected platforms completed at a cost of $342 million in 1983 — BSP's biggest and costliest project. Its main function is the secondary recovery of oil through the injection of treated seawater and processed natural gas under pressure into underground reservoirs in order to push the oil towards wellheads. Declining oil prices, however, raised fears the project might never be able to pay for itself.

Oil from both offshore and land is piped to Seria for treatment and storage at a large tank farm. From there crude is piped offshore for loading onto tankers at a single buoy mooring terminal, although some is retained for BSP's nearby oil refinery which went into production in 1984. It has a capacity of 10,000 barrels per day to meet all Brunei's gasoline, diesel, kerosene and liquefied petroleum gas (LPG) needs.

The very existence of the refinery reflects the growing active involvement of the government in the petroleum industry. From a hard-nosed profit-and-loss viewpoint, the refinery is too small to make economic sense, and besides that it takes business from the Shell Group's refinery in Singapore which had previously supplied Brunei's needs. But the security-minded sultan and his men wanted the refinery for understandable strategic reasons, as the sea lanes could conceivably be cut off by a hostile power.

The Shell Group would probably also like to keep oil production levels high, at least when prices are high, but the government as equal partner has prevailed in having a policy of conservation adopted. As a result, production dropped from a high of 240,000 barrrels per day in 1980 to 173,000 three years later, and during 1985 a poor producer's market took it close to 100,000 — still enough to pay the sultanate's expenses while at the same time boosting foreign currency reserves. Production subsequently rebounded to the target 180,000 barrels per day range although BSP had to turn to the spot market to dispose of it all, in contrast to its past history of generally being able to make long-term agreements. The oil market reflects, of course, the decisions and fissures of the Organization of Petroleum Exporting Countries (OPEC). Brunei is not a member but has been described as a sympathizer, although its marketing decisions generally seem to have been based on economic considerations rather than a desire to demonstrate solidarity.

The multi-billion dollar question for Brunei is how long the oil and gas will last. Nobody really knows, given such variables as changing market conditions, future discoveries, and the probable refinement of techniques to recover every possible drop and sink ever-deeper wells. Known reserves in 1981 totaled about 1.5 billion barrels of oil and 5.6 trillion cubic feet of gas, yet three years later they stood at about the same levels because upward revisions and new discoveries just about made up for what was removed. There is a general feeling in the industry that any more major finds are unlikely, but then one never knows with petroleum.

Based on 1984 reserve and production levels, the end may come early in the twenty-first century. In order to delay that day, just before independence the sultan introduced amendments to Brunei's petroleum mining laws which increased incentives for oil companies to intensify exploration (and also shortened the standard agreement period from 38 to 30 years). However, the amendments give the government the right to take up to a 50 percent stake in the development of any discoveries. This puts new companies at a disadvantage compared with the Shell Group, in that they would have to bear all exploration costs while Shell and Brunei, as equal partners, split the costs incurred by BSP.

On the other hand, Shell's management must be continuously nervous about the company's position in the sultanate in view of official policies "to increase the participation of the Brunei government in the nation's oil and gas industry." Although complete nationalization of the industry is highly unlikely, gradual movement in that direction is evident. In late 1986, Brunei LNG was restructured from a three-way equal partnership into one in which the government holds 50 percent and Shell and Mitsubishi 25 percent each. This change fueled long-standing speculation within Brunei that a majority government stake in BSP would follow, even if it comes to only 51 percent.

The Shell Group's uncertain position was underlined in 1982 by an apparent bid to lessen dependence on BSP through the formation of Jasra Jackson Private Limited, 75 percent owned by Jackson Exploration Incorporated of Dallas and 25 percent by members of the royal family. This was widely interpreted as a highly political move signaling an end to BSP's monopoly position.

Jasra Jackson started off by obtaining an offshore concession area of about 1,220 square miles which BSP had relinquished over the previous few years (its other concessions run through 2003 and 2007). It thus joined two other American-dominated concessionaires, Woods Petroleum (based in Tulsa, Oklahoma) with an area of 605 square miles onshore and 190 offshore, and Sunray Borneo and its partners with 385 square miles, mostly onshore.

Although these concerns had failed to find commercial oil deposits since the early 1970s, Jasra Jackson's head, Dallas oilman Melvin Jackson, confidently predicted quick strikes based on seismic survey data bought from BSP. His pronouncements sparked interest in a Jackson Exploration share offer on the London Stock Exchange to finance exploratory drilling in Brunei (as well as some operations in Indonesian Kalimantan).

Prudential Insurance reportedly joined the bandwagon by buying two million shares at £2.30 each — but the stock plunged to 75 pence later in 1983 after Jasra Jackson sank two near-dry holes. After that the company decided to do a year or two of seismic survey work of its own before attempting any more drilling, for which it hoped to get financial backing from Phillips Petroleum through a farm-in agreement. Under the agreement, Phillips was to pay for drilling three exploratory wells during 1985, but would have to drill a fourth well to qualify for 30 percent of production revenues from any finds and a further three wells for 50.5 percent. In the end, however, the government refused approval without explanation.

Jasra Jackson subsequently became wholly Brunei-owned with the withdrawal of the American partner, Jackson Exploration. During 1986, it landed a European partner in France's state-owned oil company, ELF–Aquitaine, which took a 72.5 percent interest in a new joint-venture, Jasra–ELF, to prospect for oil in Jasra Jackson's concession area. Jasra Jackson's interest came to 22.5 percent and the remaining 5 percent went to the company's joint managing director, a member of the royal family. Also, ELF–Aquitaine promised to pay Jasra Jackson $90,000 a month for support facilities while drilling exploratory wells and, in the event of a strike, between $1 and $5 million every month depending on the level of production. Through such legitimate business ventures, royal family members are able to use their privileged positions to tap into their nation's oil wealth.

The Diversification Imperative

Whether or not there are any major new oil finds, the fact remains that Brunei's economy is entirely dependent on a finite resource that will run dry in a matter of decades. There has been talk of the pressing need to diversify the economy for years, but nothing much was done about it until 1984, when the government hired a British consultant, Huszar Brammah, to draw up a 20-year plan for industrial development. Manufactured products then accounted for less than one percent of Brunei's exports; besides the LNG plant and the petroleum refinery, the only plant of note bottled soft drinks.

The future direction of Brunei's diversifying economy was outlined in its Fifth Five-year National Development Plan, running from 1986 through 1990. According to Development Minister Pehin Dato Abdul Rahman Taib, the government planned to promote Brunei as a regional banking and finance center, introduce a national training scheme to make full use of local manpower, improve monitoring of the economy, and allow private industry to take over some government services. Among steps being considered to encourage citizens to work in the private sector, which would play a key role in developing new non-oil industries, was the introduction of a national pension fund (one attraction of government jobs has been the provision of retirement benefits).

The five-year plan suggested a variety of high-value-added and non-labor-intensive industries which should be set up in the name of diversification. Potentially the biggest new industry would be a cement factory grinding imported clinker, which in turn could support a precast concrete factory supplying local construction companies. Other possible industries include food canning and packaging, furniture, textiles, pottery and tiles (made from local clay deposits), chemicals and dyes, plywood and wood paneling, and glass products. Investigation into the potential of biotechnology was also recommended. However, all of these industries tend to be oriented towards job-creation and import-substitution, with none likely to earn export revenues at even a fraction of the rate of petroleum.

The part of the five-year plan sparking the most interest in the local business community was the idea of making Brunei a regional money capital. This would seem to have more potential for earning revenues than any of the suggested factory-based industries, which face a variety of constraints despite the ready availability of start-up capital and cheap energy. One constraint is the small local market for manufactured products; the combined population of Brunei, Sabah and Sarawak is well under three million, with a large proportion living in remote areas and lacking buying power. Another is the long distance to overseas markets (although that never stopped Japan). And yet another is the lack of manpower at all skill levels. In addition, Brunei has very little in the way of non-petroleum natural resources. Besides oil and gas, the only resource of note is pure white silica sand. The sultanate is blessed with an estimated 20 million tons of the stuff, which Japanese experts, visiting in the early 1960s, judged to be suitable for optical use (a pair of demonstration spectacles was made for Sir Omar from the sand). Since then, however, the electronics and computer industries have come to run on silicon, leading to suggestions that Brunei's sand could support a high-value microchip manufacturing industry.

Then there are the forests which cover more than three-quarters of the sultanate's land area. However, unlike the forests of many other parts of Borneo, they contain a low proportion of commercially valuable timber. This has at least helped to save Brunei's share of the world's oldest and most botanically diverse rain forests from destruction and led to proposals that conservation-minded nations and organizations help Brunei to maintain this situation. The government has in the past been sympathetic to forest conservation, as shown by its ban on timber exports; domestic production of about 100,000 tons a year amounts to less than 0.2 percent of gross domestic product. The intensive development of the forestry industry therefore seems unlikely unless Brunei gets desperate.

Some forest, however, might be cleared for plantation-style agriculture, although there would be some formidable barriers to overcome. An agricultural survey sponsored by BSP in the early 1980s identified such problems as primitive transport infrastructure in suitable areas, the predominance of steep hills and the lack of workers, plus the need to leave the forest undisturbed in water catchment areas. Yet the government would like to reduce dependence on food imports, which run to nearly $100 million a year (just under a quarter of all imports) while agricultural products don't even reach 0.1 percent of exports.

The older, generally illiterate generation of mainly subsistence farmers continues to venerate the land, but their children are abandoning it for the excitement of town life. The Agriculture Department has about 2,000 under-utilized staffers who may well outnumber the farmers; free pesticides and technical help plus fertilizer subsidies are offered, but there are few takers. The sultanate still imports close to four-fifths of its rice, the staple food, despite the government's intention announced many years ago to attain self-sufficiency by 1980. Two mechanized production schemes for rice have failed to reach their production targets due to bad weather and various technical problems. The most successful farm ventures have been undertaken by Chinese vegetable growers, but again, Brunei is highly dependent on vegetable imports from Sabah and Sarawak and even Australia. The prospects for developing agriculture on a large scale are not at all promising. Brunei's money might be better invested overseas, along

Schoolgirls tending a roadside watermelon stall after school.

the lines of the 1981 purchase of a cattle ranch (which is greater in area than the sultanate itself) in Australia's Northern Territory.

Like agriculture, the fisheries industry is also undeveloped and many fishermen operate at the subsistence level. In 1984, the estimated production of fisheries products was only about 3,000 tons (about 0.1 percent of gross domestic product) compared to imports of 5,000 tons. However, there seems to be scope for commercial exploitation of Brunei's waters (the fisheries limit has been extended to 200 miles in line with the new international Law of the Sea), especially in Brunei Bay where the aquaculture of fish (in cages) and cockles might be viable. Prawn farming in ponds is another possibility.

A Brunei Malay boy proudly displays crabs he's trapped next to his house over the Brunei River in Kampong Ayer.

But it is apparent that both fisheries and agriculture are not likely to be major export revenue earners in the foreseeable future; the best that can be hoped for is that, like forestry, they can be developed enough to meet most of the sultanate's needs and reduce import bills. That leaves Brunei with its sand — but at least it's potentially valuable sand, unlike most of that of kindred sultanates in the Middle East.

Who Will Do the Work?

No matter what direction Brunei chooses for its economy, it will have to contend with a serious manpower shortage that is likely to get worse before it gets better. One revealing statistic is that close to 350,000 visitors enter this country of some 230,000 souls each year. Only a handful are tourists (there's not much to see besides Kampong Ayer, the Omar Ali Saifuddin Mosque and the nodding donkeys); the vast majority are either British or Singaporean military men or "guest" workers and their families (many make multiple entries, which also contributes to the high figure). Dependence on foreign workers is almost a tradition in Brunei (remember that in the late 1800s, Chinese were hired by the royalty to collect taxes and run trade monopolies), and it has been especially evident ever since development of the Seria oilfield began around 1930.

Employment patterns in the sultanate are revealing, with Brunei Malays predominant in government service, Westerners and Chinese at the upper levels of the private sector, and Asians from other countries doing most of the dirty work.

After Brunei became internally independent in 1959, the policy was to replace the many Britons at the top levels of government with Bruneians — but only with those who were sufficiently qualified and experienced (most were graduates of British universities). This was a gradual process, and not until independence did all government departments come to be headed by Bruneians (even then a number of British officers continue to hold senior positions). Social services were extended rapidly after the 1962 rebellion partly to reduce discontent, leading to an equally rapid swelling of the bureaucracy — which itself is something of a social service through the provision of jobs for the sultan's "people." One requirement for getting an administrative post is to be Malay (by definition, Muslim — and in Brunei, a Sunni of the Shafii school), and virtually the entire civil service consists of Brunei Malays although non-citizen Chinese and expatriates from a range of countries hold many professional posts that can't be filled locally as yet.

Nearly three-fourths of all working Brunei Malays are in government service, which has many attractions including high pay, a workload that is likely to be light, subsidized car and housing loans and, for higher levels of staff, subsidies for private school tuition, round-trip air fare to Singapore annually, and air fare to England once in a career. With about 35,000 employees — more than a third of the sultanate's workforce and close to one-seventh of the population — the civil service is clearly bloated, but it keeps the folks happy. On the other hand, this situation has made it hard for private firms to recruit Brunei Malays as desired by the government. Even BSP, the second largest employer with a workforce of more than 13,000, can't match the government's largesse (which extended to an independence gift of a 15 to 40 percent pay raise announced in July 1984 but retroactive to the start of the new year).

A large proportion of BSP's trained technicians are Chinese long resident in Brunei but lacking citizenship. The government, however, wants more Brunei Malays in the all-important oil industry, and in the 1970s began pressuring BSP to recruit and train more of them to fill top administrative and technical positions. The company has found it difficult to attract high-caliber citizens, but its protestations that it has always done its best to groom local talent must be taken with a big grain of salt. After all, the company has been operating in Brunei for more than half a century, yet with only a couple of exceptions the entire upper-level management remains British or Dutch. By the mid-1980s, when citizens had yet to comprise even half of BSP's workforce, the company began following strict staffing guidelines in response to the government's obvious displeasure at the slow pace of Bruneization. Permanent residents (mostly Chinese) were warned that promotion opportunities would be "very limited" since top priority would be given to placing more citizens in key positions.

Of course, BSP is not the only employer in the oil industry. There are myriad contractors doing everything from running offshore supply vessels to ultrasonically checking pipelines for defects. Here again, the top managers and technicians are almost all expatriates or local Chinese, although the number of citizens is gradually increasing as companies strive to demonstrate high regard for the concept of Bruneization. The BSP now has a policy of giving preference to Brunei Malay contractors, but their general lack of technical expertise and experience prevent most of them from being competitive for major contracts besides those for the supply of equipment and materials.

Another major employer is the construction industry with about 15 percent of the workforce; it is the second biggest industry after petroleum but accounts for less than 2 percent of gross domestic product. Again, the main contractors are international (Japanese, South Korean, Filipino or American) or local Chinese who employ few Brunei Malays.

As for the commercial sector, the British were quite right in their perception in the late 1800s that encouraging Chinese settlement in British Borneo would accelerate commercial development. Today, the Chinese dominate commerce in Brunei as well as in Sabah and Sarawak. Most of the businesses are family affairs and non–Chinese are generally only employed to do menial tasks. The Brunei government is encouraging more Brunei Malays to go into business by offering low-interest loans of up to $240,000 and has called on Chinese businessmen to take Malay partners and share their expertise, but has yet to pass any laws (such as Malaysia has) putting teeth into this policy. However, many leading Chinese businessmen have found it advantageous to go into partnership with members of the royal family.

Finally, an estimated 3 percent of the workforce is still engaged in farming or fishing using traditional methods. The tribespeople of the interior and the Kedayans around the capital still grow rice and other crops to meet their own needs, with surpluses sold for cash. Most fishermen are Brunei Malays.

Union activity in Brunei has generally been moribund ever since the BPP–controlled Brunei United Labor Front was disbanded in the wake of the failed 1962 revolt. One reason is that wages and benefits are exceptionally good by Asian standards even without union pressure. The only union of note is BSP's in-house one, which has managed to win some concessions for its members.

Those really in need of union representation are the foreigners who do virtually all the manual work. Most are employed by private contractors, who often find it easy to take advantage of them because they tend to be illiterate, and illegal immigrants to boot. On-the-job safety standards are often abysmally low, while compensation for accidental injury or death is likely to amount to a pittance. Yet as far as immigrant laborers are concerned, Brunei is a worker's paradise compared to back home, where they would earn much less if they were lucky enough to land a job at all.

Foreign manual workers comprise about a quarter of the sultanate's workforce, and without them the petroleum and construction industries would grind to a halt. The biggest group consists of Ibans from Sarawak, many of whom bring their families. They commonly live in scrap-wood shanty towns erected illegally, but these are tolerated as long as they are in out-of-the-way places (next to the Kuala Belait municipal dump, for instance). There are also large numbers of workers from Indonesia, the Philippines, and to a lesser extent Pakistan and Bangladesh.

Brunei's lure is such that early in 1984, hundreds of jobless workers began arriving from Pakistan. They invested borrowed money or life savings in their fares because of rumors that all Asian Muslims in Brunei before the February 23 independence celebrations would be given citizenship and jobs. This was of course absurd, and the influx only led Brunei to further tighten entry requirements for visitors from the Subcontinent. In fact, immigration overall is tightly controlled because of fears that too many migrants would cause social problems, but this also leads to a perennial shortage of manual workers.

Bruneians are perfectly happy to leave the dirty work to foreigners but have set their sights on the lucrative top-level jobs. The government sponsors large numbers of Brunei Malays plus some citizens from other ethnic groups to study overseas; about 100 graduate from British institutions each year. Many Chinese residents foot the university bills for their children, but a large proportion of them decide not to return to a country where they lack citizenship.

Now the government is giving priority to manpower training locally, with good quality ensured through the affiliation of local institutions with well-established overseas ones. Training at home not only saves foreign exchange, but sharply reduces the impact of outside influences on impressionable minds and allows their molding according to the three main principles of education in Brunei, which were handed down in 1985. Two of these principles, appreciation of the Malay Islamic Monarchy concept and the "Islamization of Knowledge," may be seen as part of efforts to maintain stability and establish a national ideology. The third principle, bilingualism, shares these goals since widespread use of Malay, the national language, is considered essential for bridging differences between the various ethnic groups. But there is a more practical element in the stress on mastery of English, which is acknowledged as a world language essential for commercial and academic success at the international level.

Brunei has rapidly expanded its post-secondary education facilities since the early 1980s, when there were only BSP's own technical school and a three-year agricultural training school (a joint project of BSP and the government) with an annual intake of about 30. The focus is clearly on technical and vocational training (which is also slowly being introduced in secondary schools). The first of the new institutions was the Sultan Saiful Rijal Technical College with courses ranging from food catering to aircraft maintenance. The even newer Brunei Institute of Technology (which opened in 1986) offers two-and-a-half-year courses in business studies, computer studies, and electronic and electrical engineering. Britain's Leeds Polytechnic was given a contract by the latter institution to help with curriculum development and provide lecturers. The Japanese government has also donated a mechanical training center to Brunei.

The centerpiece of the sultanate's educational development efforts is the well-funded University of Brunei Darussalam. It began as the Sultan Hassanal Bolkiah Institute of Education at the start of 1985, offering a two-year Bachelor of Education course taught mainly by lecturers seconded from Britain's University of Wales and University College Cardiff. The course follows the standard British format and graduates are awarded University of Wales degrees. The Brunei university was established with astonishing speed later that same year, with classes starting in October. They were temporarily conducted in Institute of Education buildings while an impressive new campus was built. The Institute of Education program was expanded into the university's Faculty of Education and a Faculty of Arts was introduced, again with the assistance of the two above-mentioned British universities as well as Leeds and Malaysia's University of Science and National University. With an entering class of 174 students, the Brunei institution was believed to be the world's smallest university. A tight watch has been kept on students from the very start to prevent their following anything other than the Malay Islamic Monarchy way. They are encouraged to don traditional Muslim clothes, with "T-shirts, slippers, shorts, mini-skirts, jeans, sunglasses, army jackets and other fancy clothing" all banned.

Official pronouncements indicate the university is oriented to the very practical goal of boosting the level of technical skills within the sultanate and producing "more versatile employees." The four-year courses are expected to include attachment to both government departments and private firms. The students, however, may have different ideas of what they expect from their educations. The choices of study of the entering class included 50 in language and literature and 48 in social science fields, and only 11 in mathematics and chemistry. Business studies and public administration were not very popular either. It will apparently take many years to significantly reduce Brunei's reliance on the technical skills of foreigners and non-citizen Chinese residents.

In its bid to overcome its skilled manpower shortage, Brunei can be expected to increasingly turn to a largely untapped resource: its women. Girls are given the same educational opportunities as boys, and if they have the strength of character they need not allow themselves to be shunted into the clerical, nursing or other traditionally female professions. A woman heads the Economic Planning Unit, and one of the first brick-laying courses at the Sultan Saiful Rijal Technical College had a female trainee. There are also women in the police and the armed forces.

Money, Money, Money

The tight manpower situation is felt primarily by the non-petroleum sectors of the economy, as the government ensures that BSP and its many contractors are able to recruit enough workers to keep the oil money flowing. But don't expect to be told where all that money goes. The government's annual budget is announced each year complete with a breakdown of which departments will get how much. But, depending on oil prices, the budget may consume less than half of revenues. In 1984, revenues were estimated at just under $3.1 billion of which the budget took only about $1.25 billion, while in 1985 the budget remained the same with revenues of $2.2 billion. The 1987 surplus was projected to be $1.75 billion.

What happens to the surplus revenues? There are two huge, separately managed lodes over which the sultan has ultimate control. One contains the nation's foreign reserves, which were close to $25 billion by the end of 1989, and the other consists of his personal wealth, which is shrouded in secrecy. In contrast to the massive foreign reserves, the Brunei currency in circulation in the mid–1980s was only on the order of about $120 million.

As already mentioned, Brunei abruptly took management of its foreign reserves out of the hands of Britain's crown agents in July 1983. This move was presaged five years earlier by the transfer of a portion of the portfolio to two British financial institutions, the Morgan Grenfell merchant bank and the James Capel stockbrokerage, which were soon joined by Wardley, the merchant banking arm of the Hong Kong and Shanghai Banking Corporation. What remained with the crown agents was in 1983 entrusted to two United States banks, Citibank and Morgan Guaranty, and two Japanese securities firms, Daiwa and Nomura. These four advisers reportedly collectively charge at least $20 million in fees each year, about five times what the crown agents had. Morgan Guaranty was apparently chosen on the advice of one of its owners, Lord Shawcross, a friend of the royal family who is believed to have been a trustee of its personal wealth.

Overall responsibility for managing the foreign reserves lies with the Brunei Investment Agency (BIA). This was created just before the crown agents were sacked to replace the Investment Advisory Board, which was dominated by British experts. The BIA's board of directors includes several government ministers and is chaired, of course, by one of the royal brothers (Prince Jefri). The managing director is a Bruneian, Dato Abdul Rahman bin Haji Karim, who had gained valuable experience serving on the Investment Advisory Board.

In early 1984, the BIA had around 80 percent of Brunei's $14 billion in foreign reserves invested in mainly European, American and Japanese government bonds and the remainder in equities, denominated to the tune of 44 percent United States dollar, 25 percent yen, 15 percent Deutsche-mark, 14.5 percent British pound and 1.5 percent Swiss franc. A year later, however, came the previously mentioned sharp shift from dollars into sterling which followed a meeting over tea between British prime minister Margaret Thatcher and Sir Hassanal, accompanied by his then-trusted adviser Mohamed al Fayed. Keeping in mind the sultan's close business relationship with Mohamed (which however appeared to sour later in 1985), it is interesting that the Brunei billions, according to press reports, were deposited with London's Kleinwort Benson merchant bank, of which the Fayed brothers are also major clients. Kleinwort Benson acted on their behalf in the $842 million purchase of the House of Fraser.

It appears that the BIA does Sir Hassanal's bidding with regard to the disposition of the national wealth. He does, however, allow it to operate as it sees fit most of the time. The agency was initially heavily dependent on the various financial institutions it had taken on as advisers, but the contracts with the American and Japanese institutions require them to train some of the cream of Brunei's university graduates. As a result, the sultanate is being endowed with its own international investment experts and will before long be able to dispense with or downgrade its foreign advisers. They may be kept on, however, to maintain financial ties with the United States, Japan and Britain which may prove useful in a crisis. But if the advisers fail to live up to what may appear to be the idiosyncratic demands of the royal family, they could find themselves out in the cold — as did Wardley, which was replaced by the Union Bank of Switzerland towards the end of 1984.

In the sultanate itself, seven overseas-based, petrodollar-seeking banks have set up shop. The longest-established (since shortly after World War II) are Standard Chartered (London-based) and Hong Kong and Shanghai (Hong Kong–based). In addition, two locally incorporated banks, the Island Development Bank and the now-defunct National Bank of Brunei, were set up on the initiative of foreign tycoons who later found relations with the royal family turning uncomfortable.

Indeed, for hotelier-financier Khoo Teck Puat, a Malaysian with his business base in Singapore, relations became quite bitter and caused him so many financial problems that he could no longer be considered one of the very richest men in the Far East. His eldest son was arrested and jailed in Brunei, and suits were brought against him and a number of his companies to recover close to half a billion dollars allegedly obtained through improper loans from the National Bank of Brunei (NBB). Khoo was feeling the wrath of Brunei's rich and powerful, who thought he had betrayed their trust developed during more than two decades of close personal business relations.

The NBB was established in 1965 with Khoo's family believed to hold around 70 percent of the shares and royal family interests the remainder. It grew into Brunei's largest bank with 12 branches and some 30,000 depositors. Although the royal family held the minority stake, it was deemed appropriate that a member should be bank president, basically a figurehead position. Prince Mohamed was president for a number of years through 1984, after which Prince Jefri took over, while Khoo's eldest son, Khoo Ban Hock, served as chairman. According to talk in Brunei, the souring of relations began in 1983 when Khoo sold the Holiday Inn in Singapore to the sultan for around $135 million — a price the sultan came to consider much too high when the hotel market slumped shortly after. A couple of years later, he paid only $85 million for the bigger and grander Hyatt Regency just across the street from the Holiday Inn.

Investigations into NBB stemmed at least partly from the collapse of another local financial institution, United National Finance. A run began on United National in June 1985 after it was learned its chairman, Patrick Chiang Chen Tsong, was also executive director of Hong Kong's Overseas Trust Bank, which had gone bust earlier in the year, leading to Chiang's arrest by the Hong Kong authorities. The Brunei Finance Ministry had to take control of United National and arrange a scheme to gradually repay depositors, some of whom would be unable to recover all their money. This experience prompted the ministry to tighten its extremely loose supervision of banks, and a preliminary examination turned up irregularities at NBB. Foreign experts were recruited for a fuller investigation beginning in June 1986. Then in November, the sultan issued an emergency order closing both NBB and its finance company, National Finance, and placing them under the control of the Finance Ministry. Even more startling was the arrest in Brunei of Khoo Ban Hock plus the bank's senior manager and two of its external auditors, all of whom were held without bail. The NBB executive director, Chen Ping Fang, was arrested in Singapore and extradited to Brunei, although he was later released on bail due to ill health and died in May the following year.

The NBB men were charged in court with false accounting and

conspiracy to defraud. According to the Finance Ministry, they were behind some $650 million in NBB loans to "Khoo-related companies" without proper documentation or security. In fact, up to 98 percent of the bank's loans were said to have gone to "Khoo-related interests." The bank allegedly financed day-to-day operations through heavy borrowing on the interbank market, mainly overseas, and only in this way could it "maintain its facade of being a profitable and respected financial institution."

On Khoo's side there was an attempt to make the whole affair look like a business misunderstanding between friends. Sources close to Khoo suggested the rupture with the sultan was linked to a royal family bid to buy a majority stake in NBB, with the subtle implication that Khoo's son was being held hostage to this end. Khoo himself issued a statement expressing the hope that "any misunderstanding can be settled amicably." He said he had received "a number of business proposals" from the sultan through his son, adding, "These matters have been taken under consideration and hopefully may be resolved to mutual satisfaction." It was unclear whether what Khoo called "business proposals" corresponded to the "negotiations" referred to by Dato Abdul Rahman (in his capacity as Finance Ministry permanent secretary) when he said the government had "tried to avert the bank's closure by conducting in good faith negotiations with the Khoos in an attempt to persuade them to restructure the loans and provide adequate security."

The failure of those negotiations, and perhaps the passing of Sir Omar and his possible modulating influence with regard to an old friend, led to severe legal action by the Brunei government. Not only were the NBB quartet arrested on criminal charges, but civil suits were filed in succeeding months as the bank's complex affairs were unraveled. These suits sought the recovery of around $475 million in loans to Khoo-related companies in Brunei, Singapore, Hong Kong and Malaysia, which had large chunks of their assets frozen on court order pending an outcome. Khoo was personally sued for $160 million as guarantor of one large loan. The Brunei government, represented by Britain's biggest law firm, Clifford Chance, agreed to the unfreezing of assets only when they were to be sold to repay the NBB loans. The primary asset Khoo was allowed to sell was Southern Pacific Hotel Corporation, which controlled Travelodge, Australia's largest hotel chain. Khoo bought Travelodge in 1981 for about $120 million from the peripatetic cultivator of the ultra-rich, Adnan Khashoggi, and sold the 48-hotel chain for more than $400 million. By July 1987, Khoo had reportedly raised around 80 percent of the money owed to NBB, but was insisting that before he paid up, the charges against his son and the other NBB men would have to be dropped. But the sultan had the stronger hand. The Clifford Chance lawyers notified Khoo's lawyers that negotiations over repayment were terminated since the Brunei government would not consider any compromise due to its belief that the men charged were guilty of massive fraud. In addition, five criminal charges were brought against the elder Khoo himself, who refused to present himself in court to answer them and is commonly referred to as a "fugitive tycoon" in news reports.

With the two sides unable to reach agreement, Brunei's trial of the century went ahead in the High Court beginning in October that year. Khoo's position became even more untenable the following month when his son pleaded guilty to two of the charges against him. Ban Hock had already spent a year in jail and reportedly hoped to minimize his time there through a plea bargain with the prosecutor, who dropped six other charges in return. Two co-defendants subsequently followed Ban Hock's lead and entered guilty pleas as well. The senior Khoo was so angered by his son's action, which put his own talk of a business "misunderstanding" in an ill light, that he fired his London lawyers for failing to head it off. Ban Hock was sentenced to four years and four months in jail in February 1988, when he was 50. The term was later cut by a year on appeal after the defense argued that Ban Hock was of good character but had been led to break the law because he came from a strict, feudal Chinese family with a dominant father whose directives had to be obeyed. As for his co-defendants, the bank's senior manager was jailed for 27 months, one auditor was jailed for 20 months, and the other auditor was set free after having spent 14 months in jail before and during the trial.

A half year after his son's sentencing, the senior Khoo finally repaid in full the final $280 million which the NBB owed to various creditors — about $210 million in principal and interest to international banks which had given NBB unsecured interbank credit lines, and $70 million to reimburse the Brunei government for covering the losses of local depositors. But sources in Brunei said the sultan remained angry at Khoo and it was therefore unlikely the criminal charges against him would be dropped. Thus Khoo seemed likely to remain a fugitive since Brunei's triangular extradition agreement with Malaysia and Singapore made it risky for him to set foot in either of the countries where he had built his fortune.

The closure of NBB left Island Development Bank (IDB) as Brunei's only active locally incorporated bank. The Bruneization of IDB during the same period when investigations into NBB went into high gear tends to support the suggestion by Khoo's side that his troubles stemmed at least partly from Brunei desire for control of his bank. On the other hand, there have been suggestions that the IDB move was meant to prevent it from being misused by foreigners in the same way as NBB. The tycoon who lost out at IDB was Enrique Zobel, whose Ayala (Holdings) Company was lead contractor for the new Istana, but his departure was much more amicable than Khoo's. Zobel, a senior member of one of the Philippines' leading oligarchic families and a polo-playing buddy of Sir Hassanal's, was the main force behind the launching of IDB in 1980 as a fifty-fifty joint-venture with the royal family. Ayala took a 25 percent interest while the Bank of the Philippine Islands (BPI), which Zobel also headed, took another 25 percent. The BPI, however, relinquished its share in early 1985 when the exchange controls of the financially pressed Philippines meant it could not move out the funds needed to participate in a capital increase for IDB to $5.4 million. A restructuring of IDB left royal family interests with 60 percent of the equity, Japan's largest bank, Dai Ichi Kangyo, with 20 percent and Ayala with the other 20 percent (and also a five-year contract to manage the bank). Zobel remained IDB chairman and chief executive, and announced plans to make it the biggest bank in ASEAN. In August 1986, though, he unexpectedly quit both posts with a bland explanation that failed to tell the whole story. "I have accomplished my personal commitment to the principal share-holders to quickly establish the bank as a leading financial institution in Brunei," he said in a press statement. He added, "I and other non–Bruneian directors feel confident in encouraging a transfer of responsibility at this time." As a result, Bruneians took seven seats on the board while Dai Ichi Kangyo Bank took the other two; the Finance Ministry's Dato Abdul Rahman was named chairman.

The Bruneization of locally incorporated financial institutions was clearly in tune with proposals in the Fifth Five-year National Development Plan (1986–1990), which expanded Zobel's grand vision for IDB into one in which Brunei would be a regional banking and finance center. Plans included creation of a monetary authority to oversee moves in this direction, and also a development bank to facilitate industrial and commercial development within the sultanate. To many observers, the goal of becoming a money capital makes more sense than trying to diversify the economy through industrialization. Brunei's foreign reserves and royal family fortunes could obviously provide a substantial lending base for the generation of more profits at home rather than overseas. Good communications are another prerequisite that Brunei is now coming to satisfy, thanks to the acquisition of modern telecommunications technology and the impressive expansion of the national airline's route network.

Brunei's expanding financial ties go hand in hand with diplomatic and trade relations. That Japanese financial institutions such as Dai Ichi Kangyo are now taking on a high profile in the sultanate should come as no surprise, for it is a land teeming with Japanese motor vehicles, home appliances and electronic goodies — almost all ultimately paid for through petroleum sales for which Japan is the major customer (it buys all of Brunei's LNG and much of its crude oil).

During residency days, of course, Britain was the predominant trading partner. That started to change during the 1960s when Japanese firms began winning construction contracts, and most notably at the end of 1969 when Mitsubishi Corporation became a joint venture partner in Brunei LNG Limited. Turning to the Japanese not only made economic sense, but also helped to diversify Brunei's economic ties as well as demonstrating an independent attitude, giving the British something to ponder during treaty negotiations.

Also during the 1960s something of a symbiotic business relationship grew between Brunei and Singapore — the two "odd men out" in those days — because the former has oodles of petroleum but lacks skilled workers, while the latter's only resources are commercial acumen and a highly skilled work force. Today, the royal family has extensive investments in the island republic's free-market economy while close links have been forged between the Chinese businessmen of the two countries. Singapore is the second largest exporter to Brunei (mostly of goods made elsewhere), after Japan and ahead of the United States and Britain. Malaysia can be expected to move up in terms of trade in coming years as it is cultivating close ties with Brunei, although the sultanate has little to offer since both countries are crude oil and LNG exporters.

By Land, Sea and Air

In view of Brunei's wealth and small land area, it is not surprising that it boasts well-developed transportation and telecommunications systems surpassed only by Singapore and Hong Kong in the region.

The sea continues to be, as it has always been, the sultanate's main avenue of trade. However, the capital is no longer the main port. That distinction belongs to Muara about 18 miles away, where a 1,405-foot long deep-water wharf was completed in 1973 to handle ships up to more than 10,000 gross registered tons. There are also port facilities at Kuala Belait, just inside the mouth of the Belait River, which cater for offshore oilfield vessels as well as cargo ships (mainly from Singapore) up to about 3,000 tons. Crude oil is loaded onto tankers through a pipeline extending about six miles offshore from the Seria tank farm and ending at a single buoy mooring terminal which can accommodate tankers up to 300,000 deadweight tons. Liquefied natural gas is piped onto special tankers which berth at the end of a jetty running nearly three miles out to sea from the Lumut LNG plant.

Many imports are also airfreighted in via Brunei International Airport just outside the capital. When completed in 1972, it had Southeast Asia's longest runway. Three years later the national government-owned carrier, Royal Brunei Airlines, went into operation with three Boeing 737 jets. Initially, all its pilots, top managers and technicians were foreigners, but their numbers are slowly being reduced through Bruneization. The airline has earned a good reputation for service and punctuality, although flights are sometimes delayed or even commandeered for the benefit of royal family members. Its first year of profits came in 1983, and the following year it carried its millionth passenger.

The delivery of three Boeing 757-200 jets in 1986 allowed the addition of new destinations to the established ones of all the ASEAN capitals, Hong Kong and Darwin. Taipei was added first, with Kathmandu, Perth, Brisbane, Japan, South Korea, and London or Amsterdam (probably via Oman or the Maldives) to follow later. Two of the 737s remained in service while the third, older plane was sold in 1988. In line with the royal propensity for gold, the airline decided to distinguish itself from the competition by installing gold-plated fittings in the first class sections of its new jets, including in the bathrooms. Another feature is fully reclining leather seats. "The Boeing company got quite a shock when we ordered leather seats for first class," a Royal Brunei official remarked. Even more luxury characterized another Boeing, an executive 727-100, which serves the VIP charter market. It is operated by Royal Brunei Executive, a company run separately from Royal Brunei Airlines.

The sultanate itself is so small that there are no scheduled commercial air services within it. There is a well-maintained and almost completely paved road system serving the highly developed coastal strip, but the heavily jungled interior remains accessible only by river, foot or helicopter, or in some areas by dirt roads which may not be passable during rainy periods. The capital suffers from big rush-hour traffic jams and an acute shortage of parking due to years of rapidly rising vehicle ownership. In 1989 Brunei was crawling with more than 100,000 vehicles to give it one of the world's highest ownership ratios — about one vehicle for every 2.3 people. One negative effect has been depressed development of public transportation so that the carless minority, consisting mainly of immigrant laborers, has great difficulty getting around.

Road links with Sarawak were long neglected due to poor relations with Malaysia, but this is changing now that the two countries are friends. By 1987 each had surfaced its part of the 15-mile route between the Belait and Baram rivers, which had been purposely left as an often impassable sand track. They are also cooperating in the completion of a trans–Borneo highway that will allow motorists to drive from Sarawak's western tip to Sabah's southeast corner. The highway at long last provides land access from the main part of Brunei to the isolated Temburong District, through Sarawak's intervening Limbang District.

Temburong's links with the outside have in the past been via water, with two basic types of boats operating commercially: covered speedboats carrying around 15 passengers and small coastal cargo launches. Many villagers own their own small outboard-powered boats, but paddling or walking remain common means of getting around (a similar situation exists for the interior of the rest of Brunei).

Temburong is much less developed socioeconomically than Brunei's other three districts. The lack of a good transportation system is a factor, and this in turn is related to the district's small, scattered population (less than one-thirtieth of the sultanate's people living on one-fifth of its land) and the absence of exploitable resources with the exception of river gravel for the construction industry elsewhere in Brunei. About one-third of the district consists of a coastal plain with deep peat soil unsuitable for agriculture, while the hilly interior (rising to Brunei's tallest peak, 6,070-foot Bukit Pagan) has soils that are not very fertile. The only town, Bangar, up the Temburong River, has only about a dozen (mainly Chinese-run) shops.

Brunei is well advanced in telecommunications by Asian standards, with about one telephone for every six people and a large number of telex machines. Overseas calls are made via either of two earth satellite stations, the newest of which was finished in 1983 and has a 105-foot diameter dish capable of beaming TV broadcasts to the outside world.

Television Brunei began Southeast Asia's first all-color TV service in 1975, relying heavily on shows from Britain and the United States which have included *Dallas* and *Sesame Street*. Broadcasts of local origin are mainly Islamic religious ceremonies, celebrations such as those on National Day, entertainment specials with local and foreign singers, or dramas produced in the modern studios. To ensure that people in remote areas can keep in touch with developments, the government early on provided outlying villages with free color TV sets. Broadcasts begin in the late afternoon and are also tuned in by people in nearby parts of Sabah and Sarawak, while Brunei residents can in turn receive TV Malaysia's two networks. Brunei also has two government-run radio stations (one in Malay and the other in English and Chinese) broadcasting most of the day, and the British army operates a service in English and Nepalese for its Gurkha battalion. Many Bruneians have widened their entertainment options through video cassette recorders. There are plenty of cassette rental shops with low rates (generally $1-2 for three days) made possible by widespread pirating of variable quality. The advent of TVs and VCRs has hit movie theaters hard and only a few remain in business.

News broadcasts almost never touch on controversial local issues, but somewhat surprisingly there is virtually no censorship of foreign news that might be deemed sensitive. For example, important elections in other countries are often given extensive coverage. A similar situation exists for newspapers and magazines, which are freely allowed in after being checked to see if there are any offensive articles about Brunei. However, periodicals which try to give an in-depth picture of what is really happening in the sultanate may not be welcome; the Hong Kong–based *Far Eastern Economic Review*, for example, was banned for several years beginning in 1983. The sultanate's only newspaper, the weekly English-Malay *Borneo Bulletin* (controlled by Royal Family, Inc.), is accurate but not very informative because it must practice self-censorship. The government also publishes its own weekly Malay-language propaganda sheet, *Pelita Brunei*.

Because the channels of information are tightly controlled locally, Brunei is a land of rumors about everything from the circumstances behind business deals to the real reasons for the government's latest policy shift. This situation is unlikely to change soon in view of official pronouncements that the Western concept of press freedom is "unacceptable and inappropriate" for Brunei's Malay Islamic Monarchy. A senior Education and Health Ministry official told visiting ASEAN journalists in 1986 that "we expect the press in this country to operate within the framework of our national philosophy. Without responsibility and accountability, our whole system of government and national security could be threatened by irresponsible and inaccurate reports in the news media."

Such concerns are apparently linked in part to alleged misreporting by "the less responsible sections of the media in some parts of the world," in the words of a second senior official speaking to another group of ASEAN journalists the following year. He claimed that in some cases misreporting "seems to have been deliberately mischievous," although often it was due to ignorance. He announced that to better enlighten visiting foreign journalists, an information service was being set up to provide them with data on which fair and balanced reporting about Brunei could be based.

Such a move was long overdue. Previously, visiting journalists were referred to a section of the Information Department which proved to be poorly named, since it was able to provide only outdated data and sketchy background information (the department, which was merged with radio and television in 1985, is basically a channel for propaganda). In addition, staff members dealing with journalists tended to be unsophisticated. In some instances they outlined what should not be printed, which of course became the focus of the writings of the visitors.

The International Front

Brunei's economic clout gives it the potential to wield far more influence internationally than most other tiny countries, and consequently it has been diplomatically wooed by a wide range of nations. Brunei, motivated largely by abiding concerns about security, has in turn been cultivating friends, especially those closest to home — the other five ASEAN nations, which formally welcomed the sultanate into the fold just one week after it became fully independent. Brunei also joined the Commonwealth, the United Nations, and the Organization of Islamic Countries (oic).

On independence, diplomatic recognition quickly came from most of the world's 168 other countries, including the Soviet Union, China and Vietnam. Full diplomatic relations were established with all the ASEAN countries, Britain, the United States, West Germany, Japan, South Korea and several Middle Eastern countries including Lebanon and Jordan, although an acute shortage of qualified staff limited the number of embassies Brunei could open.

The history of relations with various ASEAN nations has been sketched in other sections. Singapore remains the sultanate's closest ASEAN friend, based on shared commercial interests as well as a feeling of being small and somewhat vulnerable, while Thailand has long been considered a reliable source of the key Asian staple, rice. Malaysia, Indonesia and the Philippines have each earned deep suspicion at different times and relations with them have been uneven, although on a warming trend since before independence. The fall from power of Philippine president Ferdinand Marcos in 1986 was, however, followed by a temporary cooling. The reasons for this are not easy to discern, but were apparently related to suspicions that fleeing Marcos crony General Fabian Ver (the top-ranking military man accused in the 1984 murder of Benigno Aquino) used Brunei as a conduit for much of his allegedly ill-gotten gains. It is not clear why Cory Aquino's government should have been blamed, but by 1987 the two countries were again on warm terms.

Lingering Brunei distress over Sarawak's snatch of the Limbang District in 1890 will undoubtedly prevent ties with Malaysia from becoming as close as they might otherwise be. The emotive power of this issue is illustrated by the uproar elicited by a small item in the May 21, 1987, edition of the *Far Eastern Economic Review*. It was reported that the possibility of Brunei striking a multi-billion dollar deal to "buy" Limbang was discussed during a visit by Malaysian prime minister Dr. Mahathir Mohamad. Although the Brunei government remained typically mum, the report was hotly denied by the Malaysian government, and political leaders of all stripes, especially in Sarawak, assailed the magazine. The *Review* was accused of trying to poison relations between Malaysia and Brunei, in line with commonly held feelings that the Western press purposely portrays developing countries in a bad light. The magazine published a retraction and an apology in which it noted that it had received the information from a normally trustworthy source, but this was not good enough for the Malaysian government, and over the next couple of months some of its ministers repeated warnings there would be punitive action. This came in August when Dr. Mahathir filed a suit against the *Review* for defamation. It was claimed that the original report damaged his character by making it appear that he was not properly performing his duties as prime minister, and the subsequent retraction and apology further damaged his character because the *Review* referred to the trustworthiness of its source in the face of his denial of the story.

Rapprochement with Indonesia at the start of the 1980s led to little more than expressions of neighborly feelings until September 1987, when Sir Hassanal made a dramatic move to boost interdependence in a concrete way. On a visit to Jakarta, he offered Indonesia a $100 million loan repayable over 25 years with a seven-year grace period. With interest pegged at less than two percent per annum, it amounted to a gift of possibly tens of millions of dollars — a badly needed gift since the collapse of oil prices over the preceding couple of years had seriously crimped Indonesia's development efforts, which are financed mainly by petroleum exports. The loan was expected to return two major stalled projects — a toll road and an alumina plant — to viability. No reason for the gift was announced, but speculation centered on possible Brunei security concerns, perhaps related to seemingly intractable instability in the Philippines, leading to efforts to further strengthen ties within ASEAN. Some observers, though, suggested a business basis due to the informality of the sultan's virtually unannounced visit and his expression of interest in investing in ailing Indocement (Indonesia's largest cement company, part-owned by the government, which could supply Brunei's needs) and also in a hotel.

Brunei has also placed great importance on cultivating relations with two other major blocs besides ASEAN: industrialized nations which share its anti-communist and pro-capitalist worldview (absorbed largely from the British), and Islamic states which stress the same religious values and the benefits of stable autocratic rule.

The industrial power with which Brunei has the closest ties is of course Britain, which will long be counted on for military assistance against external threats. Positive factors for Britain in the relationship include a conducive business climate (notably for Royal Dutch Shell's British partners), access for its military to excellent jungle training facilities, and even support on monetary policy (many analysts believe Sir Hassanal used Brunei foreign reserves to support the British pound following his January 1985 meeting with Prime Minister Thatcher).

The United States has emerged as a close rival to Britain for influence within the sultanate. The questionable treatment of permanent residents and the lack of democracy have not hindered relations since Sir Hassanal, and his father while he was still alive, never gained a reputation for strongman tactics. About a year after becoming independent, Brunei opened its Washington, D.C., embassy in rented quarters. The option of buying embassy property was precluded by the United States requirement of reciprocity, since foreigners and even permanent residents are not allowed to buy land in Brunei.

The highest United States official to visit the sultanate was Secretary of State George Shultz, who in mid-1986 had a 45-minute audience with Sir Hassanal. During a subsequent tour of his host's new palace, the secretary of state showed an interest that was particularly keen since his former company, Bechtel Corporation, was principal consultant for the ostentatious project. Shultz was Bechtel vice-president from 1974 through 1981 (and president for a subsequent year), and it was during this period that the corporation landed the plum palace contract.

Sir Hassanal's first post-independence visit to the United States on official business came in September 1984 when Brunei was admitted to the United Nations. The sultan journeyed to New York City with his family and booked a floor at the Pierre Hotel. By the time he departed, Sir Hassanal had made a media splash and burnished his image by donating $1 million to the United Nations Children's Fund and another $500,000 to feed the needy of New York. He has since made it a habit to donate hefty sums to charity when he travels (to London and Paris, for example), and the beneficiary organizations usually express complete surprise at having been chosen. There are also frequent substantial donations which enhance his image as a supporter of Islam. In 1988, for example, he gave nearly $600,000 towards a new mosque in the Peninsular Malaysian state of Trengganu — a sum sufficient to build three mosques for the population served, according to a Malaysian businessman involved in soliciting the money, "but because the mosque is to be named after His Majesty, a large and beautiful mosque would be appropriate."

One huge donation for which Sir Hassanal of course wanted no publicity at all was $10 million earmarked for the Contra rebels fighting Nicaragua's Sandinista government. But publicity galore there was, largely as the result of the funds being "lost" in a way all too symptomatic of the bumbling manner in which some of the covert Iran-Contra dealings were run by a network of United States government officials and private arms dealers. Congressional hearings in 1987 on the Iran-Contra scandal revealed that it all began as the result of efforts to free American hostages held in Lebanon by terrorist groups sympathetic to Iran. Secret arms sales to Iran were initiated at least in part to win release of the hostages, and a large proportion of the profits were diverted to the Contras to get around a Congressional ban on military supplies to them by the Reagan administration.

Humanitarian aid, however, was still allowed, and according to some interpretations of Congressional intent, there would have been nothing wrong with United States government officials soliciting aid overseas for the Contras if it was for non-military purposes. But it was never made clear exactly what the sultan's donation would have been used for if it had reached the Contras instead of being deposited in the wrong bank account. The Brunei government, in a rare comment on the affair, even insisted that the money was never meant for the Contras but rather as humanitarian aid for the people of Central America.

In his statements on the affair, George Shultz denied involvement in soliciting the Brunei contribution but acknowledged approving the plan of his assistant for inter-American affairs, Elliott Abrams, to do so. Abrams stated in a Congressional hearing that he solicited the donation through a Brunei official during a walk in London's Hyde Park in August 1986. In response to the official's query about the "concrete" benefits for Brunei, Abrams said it would have the "gratitude" of United States president Ronald Reagan and Secretary of State Shultz. Abrams maintained that Shultz's visit to Brunei less than two months earlier had no connection with the donation.

Abrams was sharply questioned at the hearings about the possibility that American "gratitude" had extended to diverting United States Navy ships from their mission to welcome aboard Sir Hassanal, a military buff. He was given a tour of the aircraft carrier *Kitty Hawk* after landing on it in his own jet in the South China Sea. This came in mid-September 1986, around the time the United States ambassador to Brunei cabled the State Department that the $10 million donation had been granted (the money had actually been sent to a Swiss bank the previous month). Abrams, however, denied that movements of the carrier and accompanying ships had been altered to suit the sultan. He said the tour of the carrier, and Shultz's visit, were "part of having a relationship with a new country that wanted to have a relationship with us."

A well-publicized aspect of the Brunei donation was that it somehow went astray. During the Congressional hearings, it emerged that in August 1986, Marine Lt. Col. Oliver North, then a staff member of the National Security Council and a key figure in the covert Iran-Contra operations, had given the number of a secret account at Switzerland's Credit Suisse Bank to Abrams, who gave it to the sultan. But somewhere along the line the prefix "386" was replaced by "368," changing the account number into one that was no longer active at the bank. When the Brunei donation arrived, bank officials therefore deposited it in an active account of a wealthy Geneva businessman who had held the moribund account.

When the Iran-Contra story broke a few months later, there were rumors of a substantial Brunei contribution, but investigations failed to unearth what had happened to it. The mystery was solved only in May 1987 when Congressional investigators traveled to Switzerland and managed to track down the money. Senator Daniel Inouye, chairman of the Senate committee probing the Iran-Contra affair, stated that it represented the "last substantial donation to the Contras unaccounted for."

The search for the money was complicated by the fact that the businessman into whose account it happened to fall shifted it to another bank, where it earned more than $253,000 interest by the time it was traced. Credit Suisse filed a criminal suit against him, which a bank spokesman said was necessary to maintain control of the funds until the rightful owner entered a claim. The Geneva investigating judge who ordered the funds frozen said the businessman apparently acted in good faith, since similarly large amounts of money were sometimes deposited in his accounts by associates. When the true source of the $10 million was revealed, the businessman renounced all claim to it and the interest it had earned.

It is easy to imagine the angry mutterings, perhaps rantings, that echoed through the sultan's palace. It must have been galling to have made such a sensitive commitment believing it would be handled with absolute discretion, only to end up in the glare of worldwide publicity with the millions woefully misplaced. Even the sultan apparently considers $10 million to be more than a pittance and, rather than disclaiming it, a formal claim was filed. By mid–July 1987, a Brunei Foreign Ministry official was able to say, "We got back the money with interest."

Although Brunei's relations with Britain and the United States have been the subject of much publicity in recent years, ties with Japan are perhaps just as important, since that country commands fully 60 percent of the sultanate's two-way trade (the figure for the United States is less than 15 percent). One of the sultan's earliest post-independence overseas forays was to Japan. He promised that Brunei could be relied on to continue supplying crude oil and LNG, while Japan voiced support for ASEAN and its stand against the Vietnamese occupation of Kampuchea. The two countries also agreed to open embassies. Brunei's ambassador to Japan also serves as its diplomatic representative for South Korea, which has landed a number of big construction contracts in the sultanate.

Other major industrialized nations with embassies in Brunei include France, West Germany, and Australia, with the latter being the most important of the three in the Brunei scheme of things due to geographical proximity. This has been commercially exploited particularly by Australia's frontier Northern Territory, the source of most of Brunei's beef — mainly from the giant Brunei-owned Willaroo Station which covers more acreage than the sultanate itself. A number of Northern Territory companies have entered into joint ventures with Brunei concerns (mainly in building and construction), a process which is enhanced by twice-weekly Royal Brunei Airlines flights to Darwin, the territorial capital and the Australian city closest to Brunei. Besides beef, a wide variety of vegetables and dairy products from the Northern Territory and other parts of the country are airfreighted to the sultanate.

New Zealand has shown some interest in attaining a similarly beneficial trade relationship but has failed to make the requisite diplomatic moves. While Australia maintains a full High Commission in Brunei, New Zealand has no diplomatic representation aside from occasional visits by officials from its High Commission in Malaysia. It also undiplomatically dropped Brunei and Singapore from its list of nations deserving special trade concessions because they should no longer be considered underdeveloped countries. New Zealand responded to protests over this action by granting other concessions, but refused to restore Brunei and Singapore to its Generalized System and Preferences trade list and so gave the appearance of being a competitor rather than a potential partner.

While Brunei's relations with ASEAN and certain industrialized nations are motivated largely by practical considerations, those with Islamic countries are based more on fraternal feelings which provide a wider sense of identity. Identification with the Islamic world was underlined by the sultan's first post-independence trip overseas when, in early 1984, he went to Casablanca, Morocco, to attend an OIC summit. A few months later, Palestinian Liberation Organization leader Yasir Arafat visited Brunei and was given a warm welcome, as he had been in Malaysia where Islam is also the official religion. In September of that year, Sir Hassanal made his maiden speech to the United Nations General Assembly, condemning Israel and supporting the right of the Palestinian Arabs to a homeland. This has been a regular theme of Brunei's at international forums, along with the importance of settling disputes through the United Nations and adhering to its charter, which opposes the use of force – a natural concern for a small but resource-rich nation. At the time of its United Nations admission, full-page advertisements appeared in the *Wall Street Journal* noting that Brunei's two middle letters are "UN" and its nickname is the "Abode of Peace."

In view of the revelation that Sir Hassanal contributed $10 million to the Nicaraguan Contras, it seems probable that he has made contributions to other causes to which he is sympathetic. Among Muslim groups, Arafat's PLO is one likely recipient, as are resistance groups fighting Afghanistan's Soviet-backed communist regime. Another logical choice for Brunei assistance would be the ASEAN–backed coalition fighting Vietnamese troops in Kampuchea.

Of all the Middle Eastern countries, fraternal feelings are closest with Oman, which shares striking historical parallels with Brunei despite the great distance between them. Both are tiny oil-rich sultanates which enjoyed British protection for many years and still rely on the latter for military support. Sir Hassanal and Oman's Sultan Qaboos both attended Britain's famous Sandhurst military academy. When the approach of Brunei's independence called for at least a symbolic change in the structure of government, Sir Hassanal chose Oman as his model and gave the newly created ministerial posts to himself and close relatives while belittling the utility of political parties.

Iran is the Muslim country which is undoubtedly furthest from Brunei in orientation. The gulf between them reflects traditional differences in approach between the Shiite (dominant in Iran) and the Sunni (preeminent in Brunei) branches of Islam, which have been magnified by Ayatollah Khomeini and his followers. Brunei's royal family, like those in Sunni Saudi Arabia and the small Middle East sultanates, is concerned primarily with stability, and Islam is seen as a means for maintaining the status quo rather than forging radical changes in society. Iranian diplomats have made contacts with their Brunei counterparts in hopes of expanding bilateral relations but have failed to achieve anything concrete.

Missiles, Tanks and Boats

The royal family has given any brutish oil-craving countries something to think about by lavishing enough money on its military forces to give them a real deterrent sting. Internal and external security are the responsibility of four distinct organizations: the Royal Brunei Armed Forces (RBAF), the Royal Brunei Police, the Gurkha Reserve Unit, and the British Army Gurkha Battalion. The national budget released to the public lumps these organizations together without specifying which gets what, but purchases of high-tech weaponry for the RBAF were clearly responsible for security costs taking close to a quarter of the annual budget in 1980. By the end of the decade the proportion spent on security dropped to around 10 percent of the budget although there was not a decrease in absolute dollar terms.

The mainstay RBAF was launched by Sir Omar (appropriately, Brunei's first defense minister) in 1962 and was initially called the Royal Brunei Malay Regiment (a name reflecting the fact that virtually all troops are Brunei Malays, although members of other indigenous ethnic groups are also eligible to join). The name change was made on independence day to reflect the evolution of the army to include naval and air wings. The RBAF now has about 4,000 soldiers and officers, including some 200 women, who were first recruited in 1981 to do clerical and technical tasks and free more men for the front lines.

From the start, the armed forces relied heavily on British officers on secondment from the British army or hired on contract (Oman depends on British military expertise in much the same way). In 1981 they numbered close to 200, but a policy of Bruneization brought this down to about 150 by independence and around 80 five years after that. Almost all British military experts are expected to be phased out by the early 1990s. One reason for their continued presence is that the RBAF has some very sophisticated armaments, as well as a computer system which keeps track of supplies and transport, which the Bruneians are still learning to use and maintain.

The army has two infantry battalions with a squadron of 16 British-made Scorpion light battle tanks. There is talk of forming a third battalion to be based at the western end of the sultanate, but this will probably only be done if the British Gurkhas are withdrawn. The air force and navy are among the world's smallest but are well equipped. Military aircraft consisted of 24 helicopters in the late 1980s, with most of the muscle concentrated in West German Bolkow helicopter gunships with air-to-ground rockets, but pilots were being trained with the intention of putting perhaps six jet fighters into operation by 1992. Air defense is meanwhile entrusted to a battery of British Rapier ground-to-air missiles based in Tutong. The navy, which is geared to defending offshore oil installations, has more than 400 officers and men. Its sting is supplied mainly by three missile gunboats armed with French Exocet missiles which are occasionally test-fired at scrap ships at a cost of more than $400,000 per shot. The navy also has three coastal patrol boats, three riverine craft, and about two dozen assault boats.

Although ASEAN was never intended as a military grouping, its members are stepping up military cooperation through the holding of joint exercises. Brunei has so far participated in such exercises with Singapore, Malaysia and Thailand, as well as a major exercise with the British involving an aircraft-carrier task force and thousands of troops. The sultanate is considered a likely addition to the Five Power Defense Arrangement (Malaysia, Singapore, New Zealand, Australia and Britain). Singapore has for many years been sending its troops for jungle training in the Temburong District, where it maintains a camp for the purpose.

British army Gurkhas played the leading role in putting down the 1962 revolt, and a Gurkha battalion has been stationed in the strategic Seria oilfield ever since 1964 with Brunei paying for their keep to the tune of about $6 million a year. Battalions rotate from Hong Kong to Brunei every few years and consist of nearly 1,000 highly disciplined Nepalese men commanded by British officers. The number of Gurkhas in Brunei may increase sharply after 1997, when Hong Kong reverts from Britain to China and the 4,000-plus British army Gurkhas there must be either decommissioned or posted elsewhere. The future of the Hong Kong Gurkhas is of deep concern to Nepal, largely because they are a major source of foreign exchange for the Himalayan kingdom through salary remittances. The possibility of their absorption by Brunei was raised by King Birendira when he visited the sultanate in late 1985.

The Gurkha Reserve Unit, unlike the British Gurkha battalion in Seria, is directly under the command of the sultan. Its 900 or so men have been discreetly recruited over the years, mainly from among retiring British army Gurkhas and officers. The existence of the sultan's unit aroused pre-independence concern in Britain as it was feared these originally British recruited and trained soldiers could be used to suppress internal dissent, perhaps brutally. However, they have so far been only lightly armed and used to guard key government installations and royal family property.

The 1,700-strong Royal Brunei Police Force, which was formed in the early 1920s, is also run along British lines, with its officers trained in England. The Brunei Police Training Center opened in 1970 to train constables and began accepting women four years later.

A Pampered Populace

There is also a security element in the way the Brunei government keeps a steady shower of big crumbs falling from the royal table, since a prosperous populace is unlikely to grow restive. In terms of health, education, welfare and spending power, the lot of Bruneians is better than that of any other Asians with the exception of the Japanese.

Citizens enjoy free medical and health services from cradle to grave. There are two large, well-equipped hospitals, an ultra-modern 530-bed one (named after Sir Hassanal's first wife) which opened in Bandar Seri Begawan in 1984, and an older one (named after Sir Omar's late wife) in Kuala Belait, plus smaller facilities in Tutong and Bangar. Most doctors and many nurses and technicians are hired at high salaries from overseas (mainly Malaysia, India, Britain and Pakistan). There are also mother-and-child health care clinics manned by local trained midwives scattered throughout the country, and a helicopter-borne doctor service makes regular visits to remote off-the-road villages. The government also sends sick citizens (meaning that most Chinese are excluded) for treatment overseas if they cannot be taken care of locally. The families of Muslim citizens who die are provided with a subsidy for funeral expenses.

Intensive campaigns by health officials have virtually eliminated many once-prevalent diseases, including the childhood scourges of polio, diphtheria, tetanus and whooping cough. Nowadays the only cases of malaria and cholera in the sultanate are found in people coming from Sabah and Sarawak. Brunei's infant mortality rate—a key indicator of a country's overall health situation—is 12 deaths per 1,000 live births (in 1986), which is far better than those of most other Asian countries and nearly on a par with Australia's. The figures for life expectancy are also impressive at about 70 years for males and 72 years for women.

Health conditions are predictably poorer in rural areas. Brunei has expressed commitment to the World Health Organization's primary health care concept in which health resources are to be reoriented as much as possible from an urban-based curative focus to one of disease prevention in long-neglected rural areas. Although rural Brunei is now getting more attention, the actual extent of resource redistribution has been minimal.

A key aspect of the sultanate's primary health care program is the training of village volunteers to provide health education and basic treatment to their neighbors. Plans call for trained volunteers to be posted in at least 75 percent of rural villages by the year 2000, and for 75 percent of rural homes to each have a pour-flush toilet. Educational efforts in villages often focus on the superiority of modern medicine compared to the use of idols or the summoning of spirits to get rid of illness — practices which are also considered contrary to the tenets of Islam. Many villagers go to government clinics or hospitals only after sorcerers have failed to bring relief and their sicknesses are well advanced. Such behavior tends to reinforce lingering beliefs that people only go to the hospital to die.

Like health care, primary and secondary education is free in Brunei, and citizens who land places in overseas tertiary institutions are normally given full scholarships by the government unless the same training is available at home. Islamic religious education is strongly promoted, and there is a secondary school at which courses are conducted in Arabic so graduates can more readily continue their religious educations at Middle Eastern institutions. In Brunei, an Islamic religious teachers' college (named after Sir Omar) turns out men and women to teach youngsters in schools and mosques. The government also subsidizes annual pilgrimages to Mecca, the center of Islam, with about 3,000 Bruneians making the journey each year on chartered jets.

Housing is generally of high quality by Asian standards, but the government is planning to improve the situation further through the construction of satellite towns with large housing estates where citizens can buy homes at subsidized prices with low-interest loans. Priority will be given to resettling families from overcrowded Kampong Ayer, although many people there express reluctance to abandon their ancient over-the-water way of life, just as they did in the early part of the century when the British residents tried to get them to shift to land.

The high level of revenues from the oil industry also allows the government to be beneficent with regard to non-corporate taxes. There is no personal income tax and duties on imports are the lowest overall in the region, with the exception of the duty-free ports of Singapore and Hong Kong.

And what does Brunei's healthy, literate populace do with all its money? It consumes. Shopping is a popular pastime, as shown by the growing number of modern, well-stocked and busy supermarkets and department stores. The average family has among other (probably Japanese)

The Brunei government is subsidizing the development of low-cost housing tracts like this to resettle water villagers from overcrowded Kampong Ayer.

things a refrigerator, a color television (if not a video cassette recorder), a stereo system and a car or two.

If not shopping, people are likely to spend their leisure time in front of the TV, or perhaps eating out or simply driving their cars around. Sports are also popular, although facilities for the general population are surprisingly lacking (upper-level government and petroleum industry employees have access to well-equipped private clubs). The sultanate does have miles of beautiful beaches fringed with evergreen-like *aru* trees, but these are appreciated mainly by the expatriates from Western countries. The most popular sports for local youths are soccer and *sepak takraw*. The latter is a fast-paced game played along the lines of volleyball (the grapefruit-sized rattan ball may be hit with any part of the body but the arms) by three-member teams on a badminton-sized court.

Opportunities and facilities for top-level athletes, at least, are increasing rapidly, since Brunei began lavishing money on sports as independence approached to be competitive in the international-level events to which it would thereafter be invited. In the same way as some oil-rich Middle Eastern countries, the sultanate employs top foreign coaches in such sports as soccer, volleyball, track and field, basketball, swimming and boxing. Some of the best facilities that money could buy were built so that the Brunei Games could be held in style each year (beginning in 1985) as part of independence celebrations, with large contingents from each of the other ASEAN countries.

Law and Religion

Law and religion in Brunei may be conveniently described in the same section because two legal systems are in use — Islamic law based on the Koran and secular law along British lines.

Secular law applies to everyone, except for certain areas covered by Islamic law such as divorce between Muslims. Many secular laws introduced by the British residents (based primarily on those of Malaya, which in turn were derived from colonial India or Britain itself) remain on the books, although in recent years many have been amended or replaced — now generally along the lines of the laws of independent Malaysia and Singapore. For example, tough new drug and security laws include a mandatory death penalty for illegal possession of firearms or trafficking in relatively large quantities of drugs. In contrast to Singapore and Malaysia, however, there have yet to be any executions for these offenses in Brunei. In 1987, the High Court handed down its first death sentence in more than 20 years after finding a farm laborer guilty of killing a fellow worker over a woman. A pair of Iban women who murdered a child were the last people to be ordered to hang by the High Court, but they were executed in Sarawak since Brunei lacked a ready set of gallows.

Brunei must hire most of its magistrates (totaling four in 1986) from Malaysia or Singapore since local law graduates prefer to go into private practice. Serious criminal and certain civil cases are handled by the High Court (now housed in an imposing new courthouse), the judges of which are Britons who fly over from Hong Kong when the caseload warrants it.

Islamic law applies only to Muslims, with the policing done by plainclothes enforcement officers of the Religious Affairs Department. Offenders are charged in special Islamic (*syariah*) courts. The common offenses are *khalwat* (intimate contact between unmarried men and women, which could be simply holding hands), and eating, drinking or smoking in public between dawn and sundown during the fasting month of Ramadhan. A typical sentence for eating during Ramadhan's restricted hours is a fine of about $70 (the maximum fine for a first offense is $240).

The Religious Affairs Department (which deals solely with Islam) has grown into a sizable and influential bureaucracy. Many of its officers studied at Al-Azhar University in Cairo, which is considered to represent the progressive rather than the fundamentalist stream of Islamic thought. Although the sultan is of course considered the head of Islam in Brunei, the department's chief *kadi* regularly hands down Koranic interpretations to

Brunei village mosque, with typical rice storage hut at left.

guide Muslims (for example, that they should not join such organizations as the Lions, Jaycees and Rotary as these are considered Zionist tools).

The government continually stresses the need to adhere to Islamic values in public and private life — a campaign which is partly aimed at keeping the people away from politics. Koran reading is promoted as a healthy pastime, and reading competitions are regularly held by social organizations for their members and by government departments for their staffers. Annual district-level contests serve to choose the finalists for the national championships, lasting several evenings, which are broadcast in full over television. The contestants are judged for their accuracy and the quality of their voices as they soberly sing out their assigned Koranic verses. Brunei's best sometimes capture one of the top three places, in either the men's or women's sections, at the world championships held each year in Kuala Lumpur.

Islam is Brunei's official religion, but that is not enough for some Muslims who, looking to the examples of Saudi Arabia and Pakistan, would like to see an Islamic state governed according to the Koran. In this respect the government must play a balancing act, as such a move would be resisted by the large non–Muslim minority which makes the petroleum industry go, as well as a great many Muslims. In addition, Islamization could be inimical to the interests of the royal family if it proceeded in a populist or anti-capitalistic direction, or it could threaten the whole fabric of Brunei society if it took an aggressively fundamentalist tack. The sultan and other leaders periodically issue warnings against Islamic extremism, which is characterized as "deviationist" and "aimed at destroying our beliefs and smearing the purity and truth of Islam."

The Islamization lobby has had some success in getting various regulations introduced. In line with Koranic prohibitions, no alcohol is served on Royal Brunei Airlines flights; only a few retail establishments are licensed to sell liquor in the towns. Nightlife is confined to private clubs since restaurants and the few bars are required to close at 10 P.M., or an hour later on weekends; live entertainment is seldom allowed. Signs warning away Muslims have been put up in most restaurants and coffee shops because they are not operated according to a strict reading of the Koran, which decrees not only that they must serve food which is *halal* (prepared by Muslims in the way specified by the Koran), but also that the food must be served by Muslims and the establishment be Muslim-owned.

Many Brunei men once indulged in occasional trips to hair salons staffed by women who made most of their money from after-hours trysts, but in 1983 some 20 salons closed and around 200 foreign barber girls had their work permits cancelled after it was ruled that, according to the Koran, women could not cut men's hair. Imported TV shows and films (whether for the big screen or on video cassettes) are sanitized by censors who go to the extent of snipping out simple goodbye kisses between husbands and wives.

Fears that an Islamic state was at hand were stoked among non–Muslims when Sir Hassanal said in his 1988 birthday speech that whipping with rattan canes would be made mandatory for certain serious crimes. Since whipping is among the punishments used in the few countries with Koran-based legal systems, this announcement prompted talk that amputating the hands of thieves and stoning adulterers would follow. However, whipping was (and remains) a punishment option for rapists, murderers and drug dealers even in British colonial times in Malaysia and Singapore, and its introduction in Brunei appeared to be in line with the sultan's explanation, as a deterrent to crime (in Malaysia, a longer jail term is widely considered preferable to facing the rattan). The introduction of whipping would bring the sultanate in line with its neighbors rather than heralding an Islamic state.

It is worth noting that the various regulations and policies which have stemmed from Koranic impulses in Brunei may be subject to reversal. Both their introduction and survival depend on the relative power of different factions within the government bureaucracy and the trade-offs they are willing to make. During the last years of Sir Omar's life, his feud with his eldest son was sometimes reflected in religious policy shifts. The elder royal was close to the Religious Affairs Department, and thanks to his backing it sometimes seemed to function as an independent government within the government by issuing directives outside of established channels. The department's actions were often resented by officials in other sectors of the government who felt their turf was being invaded.

One case in point was the order in 1982 for Muslim television newsreaders to don traditional Islamic attire. The order was verbally reversed about three years later, after Radio Television Brunei came under the wing of Prince Jefri's Ministry of Culture, Youth and Sports which was created at independence. At around the same time, the sultan astonished Bruneians by boycotting the annual parade celebrating Prophet Muhammad's birthday and publicly chastising the organizers on television for changing past practices (their goal had been to make the parade more "Islamic" by, for example, segregating male and female marchers). These moves were apparently meant to demonstrate that Sir Hassanal, and not his father, was clearly in control of the government.

VI
A Steady State —
But for How Long?

What we know of Brunei's history and current situation may be used to outline probable future trends. How will the sultan, his subjects, and the many foreigners with vested interests deal with the problems arising from dwindling oil reserves, an anachronistic system of government, and a populace divided by rank, race and religion? Major changes in the sultanate's political and economic structure are unlikely in the next few years because the government has set a "steady-as-she-goes" course. During the run-up to independence, the people were repeatedly told that any changes would be made only gradually after a solid foundation had been established. Indeed, the present sultan, in line with the traditional conservatism of his predecessors, gives every indication of not wanting his country to develop rapidly since that holds the danger of bringing social and economic turbulence in its wake.

But Brunei, like any nation, is characterized by internal stresses that must eventually be resolved. The most obvious of these is that its lifeblood, petroleum, will run dry in a matter of decades. Although the sultanate lacks other natural resources, there seems to be every likelihood that viable income-generating alternatives will be developed. This conclusion is based on the massive foreign reserves available for investment and the government's pragmatism in economic matters.

Brunei's foreign reserves are so large, in fact, that investment earnings alone can cover the government's annual budget. Those earnings exceed $10,000 per person annually if it is assumed that the reserves, estimated to reach around $25 billion by the end of 1989, yield an annual return of 10 percent. Given that the reserves will continue to grow substantially for at least another couple of decades, it is conceivable that Bruneians could even live entirely off investment earnings. But conservative thinking and unwillingness to really share the wealth are probably too entrenched to allow for the creation of a land of no work and all play. Instead, the emphasis will

Brunei Malay men relax at a ferry landing point on the Belait River, across from Kuala Belait.

be on generating attractive jobs, which manpower experts have already identified as one of Brunei's most pressing needs.

Job generation is indeed an urgent matter when it is realized that more than 40 percent of the sultanate's population is under the age of 15; the number of job-seekers will therefore mushroom over the coming years. Because young Bruneians seem unwilling to do manual work, the government will promote the growth of financial institutions and high-tech industries initially managed by foreign experts, who will be expected to train their Bruneian underlings to replace them. The dirty work will continue to be done by migrant Asians entering on temporary permits.

The government has already started intensively promoting technical training. The foundation for this is being laid with the present generation—Brunei's first to be almost entirely literate, with the majority of students completing not just primary but also secondary school. About 2,000 are furthering their studies overseas. The next generation will be even more education-oriented because their literate parents will tend to encourage them in their studies and provide a conducive home atmosphere.

One problem, however, will be motivation, something which many of Brunei's pampered youth of today have been observed to lack; a small but growing number have turned to taking drugs. There are already a fair number of idle youths without any real job skills and an aversion to work, and there will certainly be many more in the future who won't be able to make the grade educationally. The potential for trouble is obvious: it was mainly young, disenchanted, non-noble Brunei Malays who carried out Azahari's rebellion. Brunei's powers that be no doubt realize that disaffection among youths could be explosive, but in the future the old carrot-and-stick approach to the problem might not be so easy if declining oil revenues and a rapidly increasing population (family planning is not a governmental priority) make it hard to come up with a big enough carrot. Brunei could very well evolve in the direction of a police state if discontent breaks into the open.

The current emphasis on Islamic values is aimed at least partly at maintaining the status quo and distracting Muslims from politics. It also helps to mollify those pressing for the creation of an Islamic state with all laws derived from the Koran. Such a move can be considered unlikely because there is not a great deal of popular support for the idea — and no fertile ground for it to grow because Muslims enjoy numerous benefits and have little reason to support radical change.

But there is always ample room for tensions to multiply when it comes to religious issues, and Brunei is no exception. Among Muslims themselves there is presently quiet rivalry between hard-liners and those (including most of the overseas-educated Brunei Malays) who like the way things are or support liberalization. And then there is the large, mainly Chinese non-Muslim minority which of course opposes Islamization but dares not say so openly. It can be expected that the sultan's government will continue to promote Islam but not to the extent of severely alienating any major group.

Although most of the Chinese are non-citizens, their presence is still valued for the commercial development they have wrought. The generally pragmatic government also realizes they can play a key role in helping to diversify the economy — something that in fact may be impossible without them. But it is unlikely that gaining citizenship will be made any easier for the tens of thousands of stateless Chinese, considering that the sultan did not bow to British pressure to resolve the "Chinese problem" before independence (perhaps fearing that citizenship might give them a much stronger political voice). He will keep his Brunei Malay power base happy by maintaining the present strict citizenship policy unless there is a drastic change in the situation (perhaps a Chinese exodus threatening the economy). On the Chinese side, it is apparent most will stay as long as the money flows into their pockets, but all the while grumbling about their status and laying contingency plans to emigrate.

Brunei will continue to be a peaceful and prosperous nation ruled by an autocratic (and so far benign) hereditary sultan into the foreseeable future — unless of course something drastic happens to change everything. That something could, for example, be of external origin, resulting from changing Southeast Asian geopolitical equations. Brunei has done about all it can to shield itself by joining ASEAN, maintaining a defense relationship with Britain, and building up its own armed forces.

Ironically, those same armed forces represent one of three basic sources of sudden change, the other two being popular-based political pressure and conflict within the royal family. But circumstances argue against a military coup. Officers are presumably kept happy by good pay, plenty of military hardware, and rapid promotions as British officers leave. The Royal Brunei Armed Forces monopolize the military muscle, but they are to some extent balanced by the Sultan's Gurkha Reserve Unit and possibly the British Gurkhas, so potential coup leaders would have to think twice about the chances of success. Yet one British military expert reckons that the sultan's increasing overseas investments represent a hedge against a possible military coup — something which in fact he might welcome to be relieved of the burden of governing.

There is, however, little to indicate that Sir Hassanal and his brothers really consider ruling Brunei to be a burden. If it were true, then democratic elections would be one way of shifting the burden elsewhere. But it is hard to imagine the royal family allowing any elected government to have powers sufficient to strip it of privileges. Rather, ultimate power would probably continue to lie with the sultan, with elections held primarily not to reduce any burdens but to maintain popular support for the established system and to burnish Brunei's international image.

This was indeed the direction in which Brunei seemed to be headed when a new political party, the Brunei National Democratic Party (BNDP), was registered in May 1985, becoming the first active party in nearly 20 years. Registration was apparently granted without Sir Omar's approval, contributing to his rift with Sir Hassanal. The BNDP's founders were mainly Brunei Malay businessmen and initial indications were that their political agenda would focus on gaining government support for Brunei Malay commercial advancement. It was widely assumed that, because the party had close royal family connections, it was part of plans to introduce political reforms which would minimally threaten the status of royalty.

This interpretation was supported by the release of almost all of Brunei's remaining political detainees, who once numbered around 40, during the early- and mid-1980s (most had been held without charge since the 1962 revolt, while a few were students who had agitated for change during the late 1970s). By 1988, only a few were still behind bars, and probably only had to pledge loyalty to the sultan to gain their freedom. The fate of the detainees had been considered a litmus test of Sir Hassanal's reformist intentions. However, his expressed opinion that political parties tend to bring chaos seemed all too accurate when the new party quickly split into two, with one of the resulting parties proposing radical changes and attracting a fair following. Not surprisingly, the government cracked down, dissolving the renegade organization and jailing its top two leaders in early 1988. This turn of events makes it unlikely that any political party will be allowed a real share of the power.

The split in the BNDP occurred in October 1985, less than half a year after its registration. But the first blow for the party came the day before its formal launching the previous month, when it was announced over television and radio that all government officials and employees were disallowed from becoming members. This decision was based on regulations introduced by the British in 1956 prohibiting government employees from actively participating in politics by joining or raising funds for political parties, attending political meetings, or signing petitions to the government. The BNDP had been counting on government employees to form its backbone. Since the party limited its membership to Brunei Malays, and the majority of employed Brunei Malays work for the government, its main source of members was eliminated, and fewer than 100 people showed up for its launching.

It seemed as though a search of the law books had been made for regulations to hinder the growth of the new party, with the announcement of government workers being unable to join timed to make maximum impact. Why? Probably because the BNDP, living up to the "democratic" part of its name, had been making more extreme demands than expected when it was first allowed registration. Party president Haji Abdul Latif bin Abdul Hamid and secretary-general Haji Abdul Latif bin Chuchu had made a splash in the regional press by journeying to several neighboring countries and calling for "full democracy" in Brunei and an end to emergency rule which was imposed during the 1962 rebellion: Emergency rule allows the suspension of the Legislative Council and gives extra powers to the sultan, and continues on the basis of security concerns which are no longer easy to justify.

The government's obvious disapproval of the direction the BNDP was taking helped to discourage Brunei Malays from joining, and it initially managed to attract only around 200 members. About 150 of them quit in October 1985, led by party vice-president Mohamad Hatta bin Haji Zainal Abidin, who charged that the top leaders, despite espousing democracy for Brunei, ran the party autocratically. According to Mohamad Hatta, they refused to call a party congress to decide the future leadership. The breakaway faction formed its own party which was registered early the next year as the Brunei National Solidarity Party (BNSP). Its first chairman was Haji Jumat bin Haji Idris while Mohamad Hatta became secretary-general, and its initial membership list contained 21 names. In contrast to the BNDP, membership was open not just to Brunei Malays, but to other indigenous people, whether Muslim or not. The Chinese were left with the option of forming their own party, but with only about 6,000 having been granted citizenship they can never expect to gain a strong political voice.

The replacement of the word "democratic" with "solidarity" in the name of the new party was significant. From the start it expressed complete support for the entrenched system, which it considered to be "perfect" as it stands. The BNSP's stated objectives were: supporting all government policies, in line with the concept of a Malay Islamic Monarchy; fostering loyalty to His Majesty and future monarchs; strengthening Islam as the official religion while respecting and tolerating other religions; and protecting Malay as the official national language. The party's public pronouncements tended to champion the Brunei Malay businessman, calling for easier loans for small indigenous businessmen and an end to alleged discrimination at various private firms against indigenous employees with regard to promotions. Also, in a rare point of agreement with the BNDP, it was suggested that the government should increase its stake in Brunei Shell Petroleum to at least 70 percent.

These issues did not, however, strike much of a chord among the citizenry. Haji Jumat resigned as BNSP chairman and as a party member in April 1988, explaining that the party's existence was "meaningless" since it had attracted only about 60 members. He stated that his resignation decision was made of "my own free will without any threat or favor from any quarter," obviously answering possible suspicions that his move had been induced by the government or royal family as proof that political parties are simply not suitable for Brunei. It was, after all, an odd time for Haji Jumat to give up on his party since it had gained the political field for itself a couple of months earlier when the government dissolved the rival BNDP and jailed its top two leaders.

The BNDP's unsurprising end came as the result of its continued black-sheep calls for change. One point of concern for the government was that the party was clearly having an easier time attracting members than its pro-establishment adversary, claiming to have formed more than 15 branches with more than 4,000 members. But what irked the government most was that BNDP leaders occasionally traveled to other countries where they could get publicity, unlike in Brunei where they had no mass media access at all. In mid–1987, for example, secretary-general Haji Abdul Latif bin Chuchu told reporters while visiting Sabah that independence for Brunei in 1984 "did not mean much to most people. The country is ruled by a single all-powerful person." He said the BNDP was asking that the sultan lift emergency rule, step down as prime minister, and hold free elections for a parliament to run the government although the sultan would remain as head of state. Haji Abdul Latif bin Chuchu described emergency rule as a violation of human rights because the threat to internal security posed by the 1962 uprising had long disappeared, and he added that he hoped to bring the matter to the attention of the United Nation's Commission on Human Rights. In other provocative interviews, he charged that government spending had not been properly audited since independence, and that the government made no distinction between the sultan's personal wealth and that of the nation. The BNSP did its duty by condemning the BNDP's overseas publicity offensive as "divisive."

In late January 1988, Haji Abdul Latif bin Chuchu and party president Haji Abdul Latif bin Abdul Hamid were arrested as they were about to fly to Australia. They were held under the Internal Security Act, which allows detention for up to two years without charges being filed, "to prevent them acting in a manner prejudicial to the security of Brunei Darussalam," according to a statement issued by the Prime Minister's Department. The statement explained that the BNDP was being de-registered because it had breached the conditions of the Societies Act. Specifically, it had had connections with the Pacific Democratic Union without government permission, sending a four-person delegation (including the two arrested men) to a union conference in Fiji the previous May.

Although the sultan's government got disappointing results in its first post-independence experiment with political parties, it would nevertheless like to apply a veneer of democracy. A likely scenario, as suggested by government officials, is that democratic reforms will be introduced in a way that avoids party politics. For example, village headmen, who are selected by the villagers themselves but require government approval to take office, might be called to serve as parliamentary representatives.

One fascinating aspect of the opposing stances of the BNDP and the BNSP is that they reflected divisions which go deeper than just ideology. The parties were, to some unfathomable extent, almost certainly doing the bidding of royal family members. Support for this view is seen in the lengthy and expensive overseas junkets made by BNDP leaders, who journeyed as far as some of the Pacific islands and were about to leave for Australia when they were arrested. It is hard to imagine they were paying their own ways for the sake of a near-impossible cause — and as a result much speculation in Brunei centered on who among the royal family was bankrolling it all. The total loyalty expressed by the BNSP, on the other hand, indicated that it was indebted to or the creation of a faction allied with the sultan.

Such considerations suggest that one possible threat to stability in Brunei may be emerging factionalism within the royal family. Family feuding contributed to Brunei's decline from the seventeenth century through the nineteenth. By the time Sir Omar took the throne after World War II, there was little scope for factionalism since the British were clearly in charge and other royal family members held positions that were of only ceremonial significance. The 1959 constitution gave wide powers to the sultan, and Sir Omar made full use of them to assert control. Eventually, however, his sons came of age, other aspiring relatives gained positions of power and began accumulating oil-based fortunes, and Brunei's simple backwater ambiance started to change into one of much greater complexity and worldliness. After abdicating in 1967, Sir Omar remained the power behind the throne until Sir Hassanal began asserting his authority in the early 1980s; their feud grew so intense that it broke into public and disrupted the smooth working of the government bureaucracy. One can only imagine what palace intrigues might now be in motion. Out of fear for their positions or ambition for better ones, Sir Omar's four sons can each seek allies among a bevy of relatives, who in turn must weigh the advantages of loyalty. Or else the brothers can peacefully coexist in an atmosphere of mutual trust by putting out of their minds both Brunei's fractured past and the palace coups that occasionally happen in some Middle East monarchies.

That there may be some friction within the royal family is suggested by the way Sir Hassanal organized his pilgrimage to Mecca in the middle of 1987. Also going were Prince Mohamed, Prince Jefri and several other ministers, plus wives and a variety of other relatives, leaving Prince Sufri as acting sultan. Coffee shop talk had it that this arrangement was meant to prevent anyone else taking control in Sir Hassanal's absence (Sufri being considered too feeble to do so because of his throat cancer). On the other hand, the sultan has occasionally journeyed overseas and left Prince Mohamed, considered the most ambitious of the younger brothers, in charge.

It is quite possible that Sir Hassanal himself is well aware of the danger of familial dissension, and of the importance of keeping lower as well as upper levels of the nobility satisfied. Some observers have suggested that a key to maintaining stability in Brunei will be the government's ability to provide suitably responsible positions for bright, well-educated officers, whether they be noble or commoner. It was apparently the sultan's intention to broaden participation at the leadership level when, at the end of the 40-day mourning period for his father in October 1986, he announced cabinet revisions which included an increase in the number of ministries from 7 to 11. In addition, all ministers were to have deputy ministers, which was not the case before, thus widening the scope for promotions. Prince Mohamed remained foreign affairs minister, and Prince Jefri was entrusted with the finance ministry, in which he had previously been deputy to Sir Hassanal. The sultan retained the prime ministership, of course, and took over his father's position as defense minister, but yielded the ministry of home affairs (handling internal security) to Haji Awang Isa, who has been his trusted adviser since 1971. A commitment to religious moderation was underlined by the appointment of Dr. Haji Mohamad Zain, an acknowledged moderate, to head the new Ministry of Religious Affairs. Retaining the law ministership was Pengiran Bahrin bin Pengiran Haji Abas, a highly respected and dynamic lawyer. Haji Isa is also a British-trained lawyer who has earned an excellent reputation for intelligence and efficiency. In addition to being home affairs minister, he holds the post of special adviser to His Majesty in the Prime Minister's Department, and as such is Brunei's most powerful bureaucrat. The sultan's new ministerial line-up suggests that he wants his government to develop along technocratic, but nonpolitical, lines.

Brunei is obviously evolving socially, economically and politically, but very slowly. As we have seen, current dynamics make it unlikely that any of the three main potential sources of sudden change (the military, political pressure, and royal family conflict) will have a major impact in the near future. But one thing to consider when speculating on Brunei's prospects is that, because of its small size, a change in a single element can radically alter the whole equation.

If the ruling sultan were to abdicate or die young, might his successor substitute ideology for pragmatism? Could Sir Hassanal himself become religiously inclined and impose an Islamic state? Or could there be widespread discontent due to economic hardship arising from a collapse of the world oil market? Is there a group of progressive-minded military officers already plotting to overthrow a regime they have no heart to defend because of its excessive extravagance (or because of their own greed)? Or is an Istana coup brewing in the minds of some members of the royal family who are dissatisfied with their portions at the royal table, thus bringing a return to the days when intrigue and disunity prevailed among the nobles, leading to the crumbling of the empire?

Annotated Bibliography

Blundell, Peter. *The City of Many Waters.* London: J. W. Arrowsmith, 1923. 223pp.
  An autobiographical account of Britisher Blundell's experiences in Brunei at the turn of the century when he was an engineer at a factory processing mangrove bark into cutch, then the leading export.

Borneo Bulletin.
  The only non-government newspaper published in Brunei, it is owned primarily by royal family members. It appears Thursdays in English with a small Malay language section, with separate editions for Brunei and East Malaysia. The editorial staff is constrained to practice self-censorship but manages to avoid becoming a propaganda organ of the government.

Brown, Donald. *Brunei: The Structure and History of a Bornean Malay Sultanate.* Bandar Seri Begawan: Monograph of the Brunei Museum Journal, Vol. 2, No. 2, 1970. 235pp.
  American anthropologist Brown spent half a year poring over unpublished archival material in London and devoted 15 months to field research in Brunei to produce this interesting analysis of "structural changes" over the past 150 years or so (that is, changes associated with such "perpetual" Brunei social units as ethnic groups, social strata, districts, and villages).

Brunei Darussalam Newsletter.
  The sultanate's best foot is put forward for overseas readers in this 12-page, English-language monthly production of the Broadcasting and Information Department in the Prime Minister's Office. Some articles present an idealized version of daily life in Brunei, but most deal with the form (not the substance) of the diplomatic activities of government leaders, with the names of royal family members printed in full (each requiring one or two lines of type).

Brunei Museum Journal.
  An annual collection of scholarly articles, primarily in English although occasionally in Malay, on Brunei's history, culture, ethnic groups, and flora and fauna; the first issue appeared in 1969.

Brunei Shell Petroleum. *Brunei: The Land and Its People.* Seria: Brunei Shell Petroleum Co. Ltd., 1978. 136pp.
  The sultanate's predominant petroleum entity sought to score public relations

points with this glossy general book about Brunei, dedicating it to its twenty-ninth ruler "in commemoration of a decade of enlightened and progressive rule." It is short on substance but is beautifully (and quite rosily) illustrated.

Far Eastern Economic Review.
This weekly, which stresses general as much as economic news, is widely viewed as Asia's most authoritative magazine. Every couple of years or so it runs in-depth, multi-story spreads on Brunei, one of which earned it a banning from the sultanate for several years in the early 1980s.

Haji Zaini Haji Ahmad, editor. *The People's Party of Brunei — Selected Documents.* Petaling Jaya, Malaysia: Institute for Social Analysis, 1987. 370pp.
In a 69-page introduction, this former deputy leader of the now-moribund socialist People's Party of Brunei gives the opposition's version of events surrounding the 1962 rebellion. The remainder of the book presents 41 documents ranging from the party's manifesto to a 1975 United Nations General Assembly resolution calling for "free and democratic elections" in Brunei.

Hamzah, B. A. *Oil and Economic Development Issues in Brunei.* Research Notes and Discussions Paper No. 14. Singapore: Institute of Southeast Asian Studies, 1980. 34pp.
Hamzah, a university professor in Malaysia, takes a critical approach in analyzing how Brunei Shell Petroleum evolved into a state within a state (a source of "political embarrassment" for Great Britain) and how this situation affects Brunei's overall economic development.

Horton, A. V. M. *The British Residency in Brunei, 1906–1959.* Hull, England: Centre for South-east Asian Studies, University of Hull, 1984. 95pp.
A balanced, scholarly description of the historical reasons for the establishment of the British Residency in Brunei, its mode of operation, and its achievements and shortcomings.

Irwin, Graham. *Nineteenth-Century Borneo: A Study in Diplomatic Rivalry.* Singapore: Donald Moore, 1955. 251pp.
This book, based on Graham's doctoral dissertation for Cambridge University, covers the period 1809–1888 when the maneuverings of various colonial powers produced the division of Borneo which remains today. It is a work less detailed and more readable, although more limited in scope, than the more recent one of Nicholas Tarling (described on p. 162) which deals with much the same topic.

Nicholl, Robert, editor. *European Sources for the History of the Sultanate of Brunei in the Sixteenth Century.* Brunei Museum Special Publication No. 9. Bandar Seri Begawan: Brunei Museum, 1975. 104pp.
A compilation of English translations of European (mainly Spanish and Portuguese) descriptions of the earliest contacts with the Brunei sultanate. The 115 texts — primarily official letters, journal entries and extracts from history books — must be read with a critical eye since they tended to be written by people with many misconceptions and their own agendas.

St. John, Spenser. *Life in the Forests of the Far East; or Travels in Northern Borneo.* 2 vols. London: Smith, Elder, 1862.

St. John, a close associate of James Brooke, is often credited with being the most perceptive, least ethnocentric observer of northern Borneo among the growing number of Britishers in the mid-nineteenth century. These volumes were reprinted in 1974 by the Oxford University Press as part of its "Oxford in Asia" series.

Sarawak Museum Journal.

One of Southeast Asia's oldest and best-known museum journals, this annual publication occasionally includes articles on Brunei.

Singh, D. S. Ranjit. *Brunei 1839–1983: The Problems of Political Survival.* Singapore: Oxford University Press, 1984. 260pp.

In this thoroughly documented book, a Malaysian historian examines events from the Brunei point of view and shows how past sultans dealt with internal and external pressures in ways that ensured the sultanate's survival. Important treaties are reproduced in the appendix.

Tarling, Nicholas. *Britain, the Brookes and Brunei.* Kuala Lumpur: Oxford University Press, 1971. 578pp.

A prolific expert on the history of British involvement in Southeast Asia has written what would appear to be the complete treatise on early British involvement in northern Borneo. It is so full of names, dates and other details that it is not easy reading, but it does fully present the fascinating story of the Brooke family which ruled Sarawak for over a century.

Index

Boldface numbers refer to photographs.